Victorian and Edwardian
SYDNEY
from old photographs

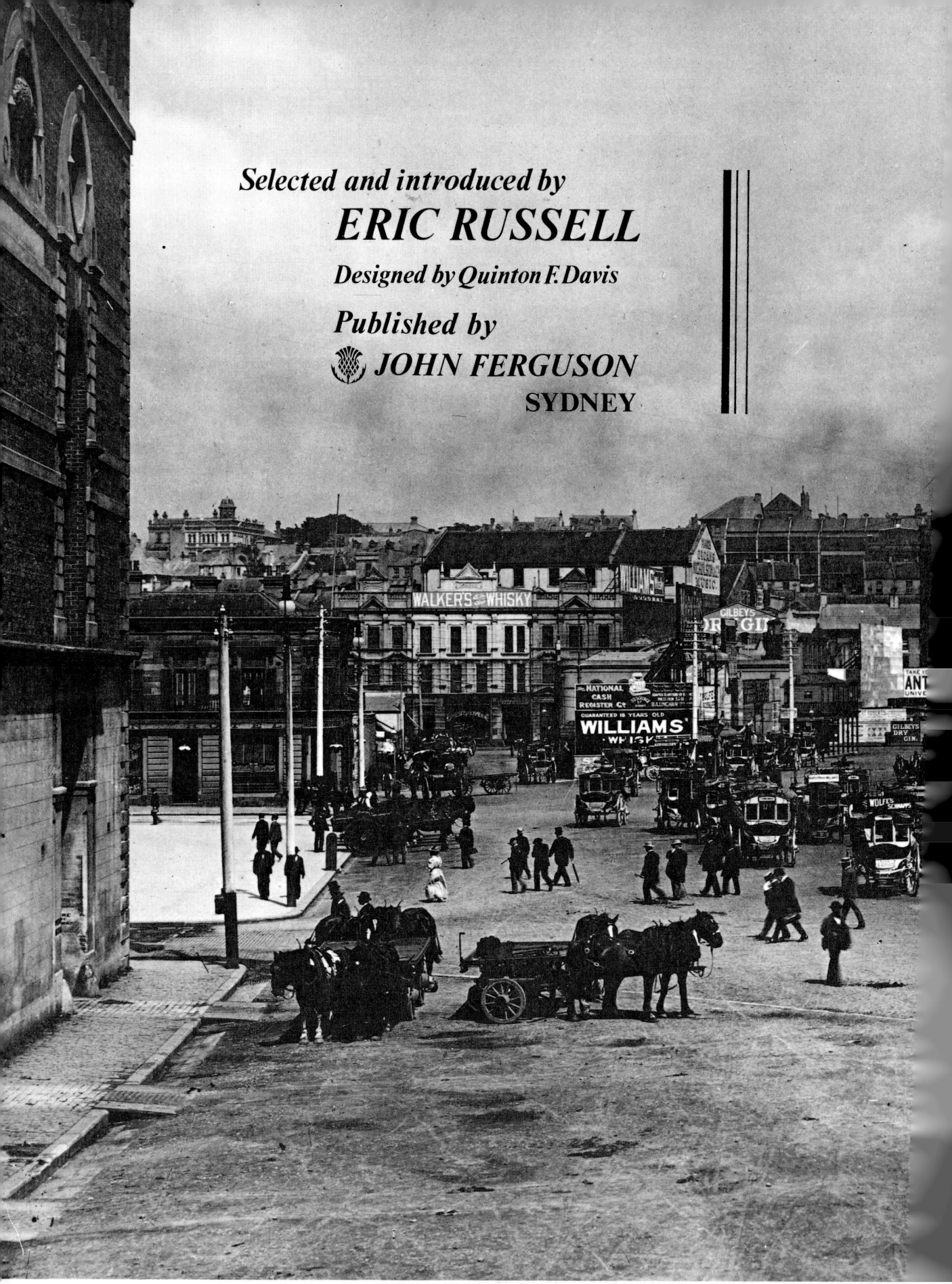

Selected and introduced by
ERIC RUSSELL
Designed by Quinton F. Davis

Published by
JOHN FERGUSON
SYDNEY

Victorian and Edwardian SYDNEY from old photographs

First published in 1975 by
JOHN FERGUSON PTY LTD
125 Mona Vale Road, St. Ives,
N.S.W. 2075

© Text Eric Russell 1975

ISBN 0 909134 00 6

Wholly set up and printed in Australia by
Hogbin, Poole (Printers) Pty Ltd, Redfern, N.S.W. Australia

CONTENTS

	Page
Acknowledgments	vi
An Introduction to Yesterday	vii

The Photographs

	No.
Playing in the back lane, 1913 (Half-title)	1
A windy day at Circular Quay, 1880's (Title opening)	2
The City	3-51
Out in the Suburbs	52-85
Emporiums and Shops	86-118
Disasters, Events, and Occasions	119-134
Sydneysiders at Work	135-157
Theatres, Hotels, Pubs.	158-168
Public Transport	169-177
A Few Sydneysiders	178-199

ACKNOWLEDGMENTS

THE MAKING OF THIS BOOK was very much a co-operative venture. In particular I acknowledge the parts played by John Ferguson and Quinton (Bill) Davis, whose contributions made all the difference. In gathering photographs and facts for inclusion I received practical help and understanding from Miss Jean Dyce, Assistant Mitchell Librarian, and Miss Yvonne Brown and Miss Jenny Broomhead, also of the Mitchell Library, Sydney; Miss Judy Allan, Library of New South Wales; Mr. John Flint, Librarian, Municipality of Willoughby; Mr. Gerald Fisher, University of Sydney Archives; Mr. L. P. Carter, Town Clerk, City of Sydney; Mr. John Olsen, Historical Section, Australia Post, Sydney; Mr. Bill Tyrrell, Tyrrell's Book Shop Pty. Ltd. (he supplied Charles Kerry's cover photograph); Freeman Studios, Sydney; David Jones Ltd.; Farmer & Co. Ltd.; Grace Bros. Pty. Ltd.; Mark Foy's Ltd.; Nock & Kirby Ltd.; Bank of N.S.W. Archives Department; and the Kanematsu Memorial Institute, Sydney Hospital. Negatives produced by the capable staff of the Photographic Department, Library of New South Wales, made possible the reproduction of material from the libraries. Among others whose help was much appreciated were Mr. J. B. Griffin, Director, Retail Traders' Association of N.S.W.; Mr. Harry Woodward; Mr. M. B. Hordern; Miss Dianne Patenall; Mr. George Clark; Mr. Roy Gole; Mr. Francis Foy; Mrs. Olive Nicoll; Mr. George Ferguson; Miss Helen Scarlett; Mr. W. Windeatt; Mr. Alastair Robertson; Mr. John Harris; Miss Elisabeth Hughes; and Mr. John Earnshaw.

THE SOURCES of the illustrations include the following: The Mitchell Library, Sydney (3, 4, 5, 9, 13, 14, 15, 16, 17, 23, 24, 27, 28, 29, 39, 41, 42, 45, 46, 47, 48, 50, 64, 67, 68, 69, 77, 79, 83, 90, 91, 124, 125, 126, 128, 131, 142, 151, 153, 154, 158, 159, 161, 164, 165, 166, 168, 170, 171, 174, 175, 182, 183, 184, 185, 186, 187, 188, 189, 197); University of Sydney Archives (12, 52, 53, 54, 55, 56, 78, 120, 121, 143, 199); Tyrrell's Book Shop Pty. Ltd., Pacific Highway, Crow's Nest, N.S.W. (7, 10, 18, 26, 36, 37, 49, 61, 62, 75, 76, 82, 163, 167, 176, 177); Historical Section, Australia Post, Sydney (19, 25, 148, 149, 151, 152, 153, 154); Willoughby Municipal Library, Chatswood, N.S.W. (30, 31, 135, 136, 169); Freeman Studios, George Street, Sydney (192, 193, 195); Goodman Brothers Photographics Pty. Ltd., Willoughby Road, Crow's Nest, N.S.W. (94, 160); and contemporary periodicals held in the Mitchell Library and the Library of New South Wales, Sydney. Title opening from N.S.W. Government Printer. Permission to use photographs in this book should be obtained from the copyright owners.

AN INTRODUCTION TO YESTERDAY

SYDNEY CAME OF AGE officially in 1842—the fifth year of Queen Victoria's reign—when Governor Gipps declared the town to be a city, and appointed the first municipal council. A population of 29,973 had been recorded by the Census of 1841. Great social and economic changes took place during Victoria's "sixty glorious years", and Edward VII's reign (1901-10) saw the title of Lord Mayor bestowed upon the chief magistrate of the city.

This book attempts to show something of the life and times of Sydney and its suburbs during the two periods that ended with the outbreak of the futile war to end war. It is really no more than a glimpse: space was limited; some photographs were unsuitable for reproduction, even with today's advanced processes and skilled camera operators; and copyright restrictions prevented many photographs being considered.

SYDNEY'S POPULATION increased steadily during the nineteenth century: from 10,815 in 1828 it had reached 35,358 by 1846; each Census recorded further increases:

1851 ...	44,240	1881 ...	99,857
1856 ...	53,358	1891 ...	106,938
1861 ...	56,394	1901 ...	111,253
1871 ...	74,423	1911 ...	119,711

People lived outside the boundaries of the town long before the outer districts became suburban; in the 1790s parcels of land were granted for settlement on the North Shore, and at Homebush, Concord, and Five Dock; in 1810, during his official tour of the settled districts, Governor Macquarie inspected agricultural settlements at Banks Town, Field of Mars (now Epping-Ryde), and Concord. In 1844 land at Hen and Chicken Bay, Drummoyne, was advertised as "suburban". By 1851 Balmain, Glebe, Paddington, and Redfern had populations of more than 1,000; lesser numbers lived at Camperdown, Canterbury, Chippendale, and St. Leonards (now North Sydney). The suburbs grew apace: from 9,684 in 1851 to over 60,000 twenty years later; and the Census of 1881 counted 106,374 inhabitants of the municipalities outside Sydney. John Ryan, who compiled that Census, made this comment:

> ... as time advances the suburbs must of necessity extend, and the population proportionately increase, while the City will be unable to afford further accommodation for her

residents. The limits of the City have long been too circumscribed to give house-room for more than one-half of those who get their livelihood within her boundaries.

Local government of a kind was in being outside the town as early as the 1840s; the City of Sydney was incorporated, with its own elected municipal council, in 1842; and in 1858 the Municipalities Act extended local government to any town or rural district upon petition from 50 resident householders. People in the outer districts in the 1840s were pioneers even if theirs was not a spectacular frontier of trackless deserts or great mountains. Five Dock residents complained to Governor Bourke in 1846 that their most important road had not been repaired for 14 years, and was partly impassable. In the 1870s the New South Wales Government was bombarded with huge petitions from the North Shore about the dangerous state of the Lane Cove Road (now called the Pacific Highway).

PUBLIC TRANSPORT came into being as the population spread and increased. Mail coaches and passage boats about the 1820s, ferries and horse-drawn omnibuses later, with the hansom cab. Anthony Trollope, the English novelist, here in the early 1870s, said: "the Sydney hansoms are the very best cabs in the world"; but a French visitor in the Nineties asked why there were no cabs holding more than two people:

> If you happen to be three or four going to a ball or a theatre, you must take two cabs; if you have to go to the station with six trunks you must take six cabs. Sydney is probably the only important town in the world that has no public carriages with four places.

A horse-tram ran briefly in Pitt Street, and in 1879 the steam tramway appeared on the scene: Redfern railway terminus to Hunter Street via Elizabeth Street, taking passengers to the International Exhibition in the Domain near Macquarie Street. It proved so popular that Parliament authorized 15 more lines the following year, the first being to Randwick Racecourse. Over the next two decades steam trams conveyed passengers to and from their suburban destinations with timetable regularity. Of course, those in a hurry "shot through like a Bondi tram" on the steam express-service. Cable trams operated at Milson's Point in 1886; the King Street cable line to Edgecliff was inaugurated in 1894.

The success of experiments with new electric tramcars was to revolutionize Sydney's public transport; it prompted the Railway Commissioners to convert the tramways to electric traction; a change resulting in more flexible operation, faster services, and lower operating costs. The first electric line, from Circular Quay to Pyrmont via George Street, opened on 7th December 1899. On that day travel was free, and the trams carried some 40,000 passengers; a week later 55,000 paid their fares. No wonder, in 1908, the editor of the popular *Town & Country Journal* could say:

> Even as things are at present Sydney possesses one of the best—if not absolutely the best—tramway system in the world, and the absence of accidents, considering the narrow thoroughfares, is undeniable evidence of wonderfully careful management.

Ferry services on the Harbour and up the Lane Cove and Parramatta Rivers went through something of a boom as people began to settle in waterside suburbs. The Parramatta Steam Packets (fares: 1s. 6d. cabin; 1s. 0d. steerage) called regularly at Abbotsford and Kissing Point in 1851; in the 1860s and later Charles Jeanneret's steamers served 15 wharfs along the Parramatta River; and Monsieur Joubert's ferries went up the Lane Cove as far as Fig

Tree. There were also ferries to Milson's Point, Manly, Balmoral and other lower North Shore places, and to the harbour-side Eastern Suburbs.

THE OPENING OF THE MITCHELL LIBRARY, Macquarie Street, in 1910, was a significant event for Edwardian Sydney. David Scott Mitchell (1836-1907) first offered his priceless Australiana collection to the State in 1898; it was accepted gratefully by the New South Wales Government, but no action was taken to build a library to house it. By 1905 the value of Mitchell's gift and the possibility of New South Wales losing it seemed to have dawned on the politicians. A parliamentary Standing Committee on Public Works was asked to report on a proposed building. George Robertson, Sydney bookseller and publisher, warned the committee of the danger of delay, and added:

> The general public, no doubt, thinks of the Mitchell Library as a collection of books; but if every printed book in it were put away, the manuscripts, the autograph letters, the portraits, the views and pictures, the proclamations and broadsides, the maps and charts, the coins and tokens and medals, the miniatures, would still form a princely gift and one well worthy the proposed building.

He added that the value of Mitchell's collection was what it would be worth to New South Wales and to the world at large, "not what a Carnegie or a Pierpont Morgan would be willing to give for it". And to drive the point home:

> When the American libraries, some of them so wealthy that they are at their wit's end to know how to spend their revenue, turn their attention to Australiana, you will deem yourselves fortunate to have put so much beyond their reach. At present they are sweeping up the treasures of Great Britain and Europe.

To a member of the Public Works Committee who said that he believed Mitchell's to be the best Australian collection of books in the world, Robertson replied: "When I hear the money value of the Mitchell Collection spoken of, I always feel tempted to break the peace."

> Whatever its value now, the time will arrive when from all parts of the world men will come to consult it. It is no small distinction to have conferred on your city, this. Its present value is great and real; a hundred years hence one might as well offer to purchase the Bodliean at Oxford as the Mitchellian here.

Mitchell did not live to see the building completed; the Government was too slow for that. But Robertson's forecast has been confirmed by events.

PALATIAL HOTELS AND CORNER PUBS were another by-product of the growth of the city. The Australia, Metropole, Grosvenor, Wentworth, Aaron's Exchange, the Empire, Tattersall's, and others, took their places with older hostelries like the Oxford (King Street), Petty's (York Street), and the Royal (George Street).

George Adams (1839-1904) is remembered for his Marble Bar in Tattersall's Hotel, 305 Pitt Street; for "Tatt's", the sweepstake he inaugurated with the Sydney Cup of 1881; and for the "silver grills" served in his hotel restaurants. Born at Sandon, Hertfordshire, England, he came to Australia with his three brothers in 1855. His many interests included a colliery at Bulli, gold-mining ventures, the Palace Theatre (built 1896), electric power stations, a paper mill at Botany, and a Tasmanian brewery. His famous Marble Bar was designed by architect Varney Parkes, son of Sir Henry Parkes, and built by Stuart Bros.; Julian Ashton designed the stained glass; and Farmer & Co. furnished it.

The old Oxford Hotel, at the top of King Street, claimed Robert Louis Stevenson as a welcome guest; he came there initially after suffering off-hand treatment from a bigger establishment. Stevenson's party arrived at the big hotel in island attire, the world-famous author himself wearing an unpressed suit that had been six months in a box; they carried cedar chests tied up with rope, native wooden buckets, palm-leaf baskets, rolls of tapa cloth, and an assortment of coconut shells and calabashes. The manager sent them up to a small room on the fourth floor. Next day the Press reported Stevenson's arrival in Sydney, and the big hotel was forced to send all his letters around to the Oxford. Their manager made a personal apology, and begged R.L.S. to return as a non-paying honoured guest. But the novelist refused, and thereafter always stayed at the Oxford.

HENRY LAWSON brings to life parts of Sydney and Blue's Point that he knew before the first World War, in his "Elder Man's Lane" short stories. We see the respectable Johnson slinking into town on the horse-ferry late one morning after going home roaring drunk the previous night on the Lavender Bay ferry. Benno, the amiable bottle-oh, takes his cart slowly up Blue's Point Road, "the cruellest hill in Australia for horses"; and Ah Soon, an old Chinese, delivers vegetables three times weekly.

In "The Kids", Lawson introduces the Blue's Point children, who prospected for driftwood, old bottles, lumps of coal, butter boxes, and fruit cases, near the horse-ferry landing and the government wharf, or perhaps found a pumpkin fallen from a produce cart. Sometimes they went as far away as Berry's Bay or Kirribilli. The boys dragged their loads on home-made billy carts to shabby little weatherboard houses at the back of North Sydney, where there was a use for everything. His story "Going In" deals with a completely different world—a journey through the city streets inside Black Maria, the police van, to Darlinghurst Gaol, from the Water Police Station.

BUBONIC PLAGUE—the dreaded Black Death of the Middle Ages—came to Sydney in the summer of 1900; its first victim was a lorry driver at the Central Wharf, who was

> ... suddenly seized with giddiness, headache, and stomachic pains, and four hours later with a pain in the left thigh near the groin, where there was a continuously aching lump, succeeded by fever, thirst, and a bounding pulse.

It was first thought that the patient had contracted the disease from cargo carried by a ship that had called at the plague-infected ports of Bombay and Hong Kong. But the health authorities found another possible cause: the defective sewerage and drainage system within the city limits; one dead-end lane off Sussex Street, described as "a disgrace to any civilized city", was immediately opposite the house where the second plague victim died.

William Morris (Billy) Hughes remembered public reaction in his *Policies and Potentates*; of how

> Before noon, alarm bordering on panic had spread throughout the community, and by nightfall the trains to the mountains were crowded with citizens fleeing from the infected city. The columns of the Press were full of stories well calculated to arouse the fears of the people.

At first there had been only a small response to government offers of free inoculation. However,

Dr. Frank Tidswell, Principal Assistant Medical Officer, commented that, when cases continued to crop up

> ... the number of applicants suddenly increased. In the course of a week or two the offices would not hold all the crowds that collected. The corridors, staircases, and approaches were jammed with people struggling to reach the inoculators; damaging each other and smashing the furniture and fittings of the office.
>
> Members of the staff who were outside could not get in, and those who were inside could not get out; the conduction of any other business was out of the question. The affair culminated in the office being cleared by the police and the operations being transferred to a large exhibition building, with a police guard to control the assemblage.

Free inoculations were then restricted to residents in or near infected areas, but even under these conditions more than a thousand people were treated each day.

Plague victims and their families were taken to the quarantine station at North Head. Affected parts of the city area were quarantined and the inhabitants kept behind barricades; houses and backyards were whitewashed, fumigated, and disinfected; dredges excavated filth from the bed of the harbour, wharfs were cleared of rotten timber and rubbish; streets were hosed down by the pumping engines of the Fire Brigade (especially in the Rocks and along Kent and Sussex Streets); and an intensive campaign begun against rats, whose fleas carried the disease:

> Seven hundred and fifty tons of debris were removed out of the yards and houses the very first day and punted off to sea. An immense collection of old timber, bagging, bedding, hencoops, and fowl-houses, were burnt on the streets.... All old structures, disreputable out-houses and filthy stables, were either razed to the ground or destroyed by fire. Wooden floors and planking were taken up and an enormous accumulation of filth and dead rats was removed.

The plague was defeated, with a relatively small number of deaths. One of the men who played a major role in the campaign against it was John Ashburton Thompson, a London-born doctor who came to New South Wales for his health's sake. He was chief medical officer of the State, president of the Board of Health, and a distinguished epidemiologist. Sydneysiders are greatly indebted to him: with Premier George Reid in the 1890s he created the public health service of New South Wales; and the pure food acts of all the States are based on a code formulated by him.

VISITORS WHO CRITICIZED SYDNEY, calling it a dirty city, were themselves criticized in 1908 by the *Town & Country Journal*, which declared that such globe-trotters forgot that their own towns had "an infinitely better claim to such a title". However, a German traveller, Friedrich Gerstaecker, who was here in the early 1850s, was more balanced; he thought Sydney had "a decidedly English character",

> ... numerous omnibuses pass along all day from one part of the town, along George Street, to another; and besides these you find a most elegant kind of cab in nearly every street. Bread and vegetable carts meet your eye wherever you look, light milk-carts rattle through the streets early in the morning, and their bells summon housemaids to the door. "Hot pies, penny a-piece!" are loudly offered, nearly at every street corner. Fishmongers drag their hand trucks through the crowd, and fruit stalls ... are everywhere to be seen. ...

He was struck by the number of dram shops and grog-shops, adding: "drunken men and women you meet nearly everywhere". W. S. Jevons, an Englishman working at the Mint, divided Sydneysiders into three social ranks in 1858,

> ... of which, the first ... includes all who may be termed gentlemen and ladies, including mercantile men, clerks, & other chief employees, professional men, chief shopkeepers,

independent gentlemen, etc. The second class... includes most mechanics or skilled artizans, shopkeepers, shopmen, etc. The third, or remaining class... comprises labourers and the indefinable lower orders.

That tireless traveller, Anthony Trollope, found Sydney in the 1870s "pleasant and interesting" and liked its irregular street pattern:

No arithmetic will set the wanderer right in Sydney; —and this, I think, is a great advantage. I lived at $213\frac{1}{2}$ in a certain street, and the interesting number chosen seemed to have no reference to any smaller numbers. There was no 1, 5, or 20 in that street. If you live at 213 in Philadelphia, you know that you are three doors from Two Hundred and Ten Street on one side, and seven from Two Hundred and Twenty Street on the other. Information conveyed to me in that manner is always useless. I forget the numbers which I should remember, and have no aid to memory in the peculiarity either of the position or the name.

Léon Paul Blouët, a Frenchman who was here in the Nineties, found on landing that those who met him did not ask what kind of passage he had, or how he was, but

... "What do you think of the harbour?" Some journalists, too, have come to welcome us. They crowd around, crying in chorus, "Well, and what do you think of the harbour?" It is evident that this harbour business is going to be terribly overdone. "Your harbour is a beauty; no one denies that," I felt inclined to explain. "But, after all, you did not make it." I hope I am not going to be pursued and overpowered with Sydney Harbour, for I want to keep it as one of my finest souvenirs of travel.

Perhaps Trollope should be allowed to have the last word:

Sydney, to the ordinary traveller who generally forms his judgment from his eye, is a much more prepossessing city than Melbourne. This sentence, should it ever reach Melbourne, will subject me to heavy censure, as the jealousy between the towns, as between the colonies of which they are the capitals, is very great; but no stranger who has seen both will doubt the truth of the assertion.

THE CITY

3] Phillip Street, just north of Bridge Street, looking to Circular Quay East. Taken in the days of gas street-lamps and sandstone kerbs and gutters, before the electric tram and the horseless carriage. At the end of the street is Goldsborough Mort's wool store, a familiar landmark for well over half a century.

4] Sydney Cove, 1877. Taken from above Dawes Battery, looking south towards the semi-circular quay from which that area took its name. At right is Campbell's Wharf, built in the first place by Robert Campbell, a pioneer merchant who came from Calcutta in 1798.

5] Macquarie Street, northern end, looking towards Bennelong Point, 1880s. This part of the street concerned itself with ships and warehouses and bonded stores. On both sides of the street are wagons loaded with bales of wool. At right is the Botanic Gardens.

6] At the rear of Gloucester Street in the Rocks area, where the backyards of some houses also served as the roofs of those below them.

7] Late afternoon at Miller's Point, about 1902. The left-hand part of a Charles Kerry panoramic photograph taken from Observatory Hill, looking north to Milson's Point railway terminus on the North Shore (For the right-hand part *see* No. 18). Through the middle of the photograph runs Lower Fort Street. Holy Trinity, the Garrison Church, with some of its stonework unfinished, is at the corner of Argyle Street. The electric tram service was extended along George Street North and Lower Fort Street

to Argyle Place in 1901, bringing direct transport to the City proper.
At the north end of Lower Fort Street can be seen the tree-lined Point named after William Dawes, lieutenant of Marines with the First Fleet. Here he set up in 1788 a primitive, but well-equipped observatory, to make astronomical observations for the Board of Longitude in England. Dawes himself called it Point Maskelyne, after the then Astronomer Royal. Generations of Sydneysiders have decided otherwise.

8] John Simpson's grocery, 118 Cumberland Street (later York Street North, then Cumberland Street again from 1974), on the corner of Cribb's Lane, 1900. Opposite was John Murray's Australian Hotel. The pick and shovel on Simpson's fanlight suggests that he had been a miner.

9] Pitt Street at the corner of Rowe Street, 1884. Two forlorn-looking stone shops from earlier times await the demolisher. But where are Waugh's Baking Powder and Sanders' Eucalypti Extract today? Is Bates' Dandelion Coffee still good for indigestion?

10] Queen's Court, 1904. A blind alley, it ran 30 feet north off Queen's Place (now Dalley Street) ending in a stone wall behind Nock & Kirby's old store in lower George Street.

11] Malcolm's Lane about 1901. A dog-leg dead-end off the eastern side of George Street opposite Jamison Street, it was once residential.

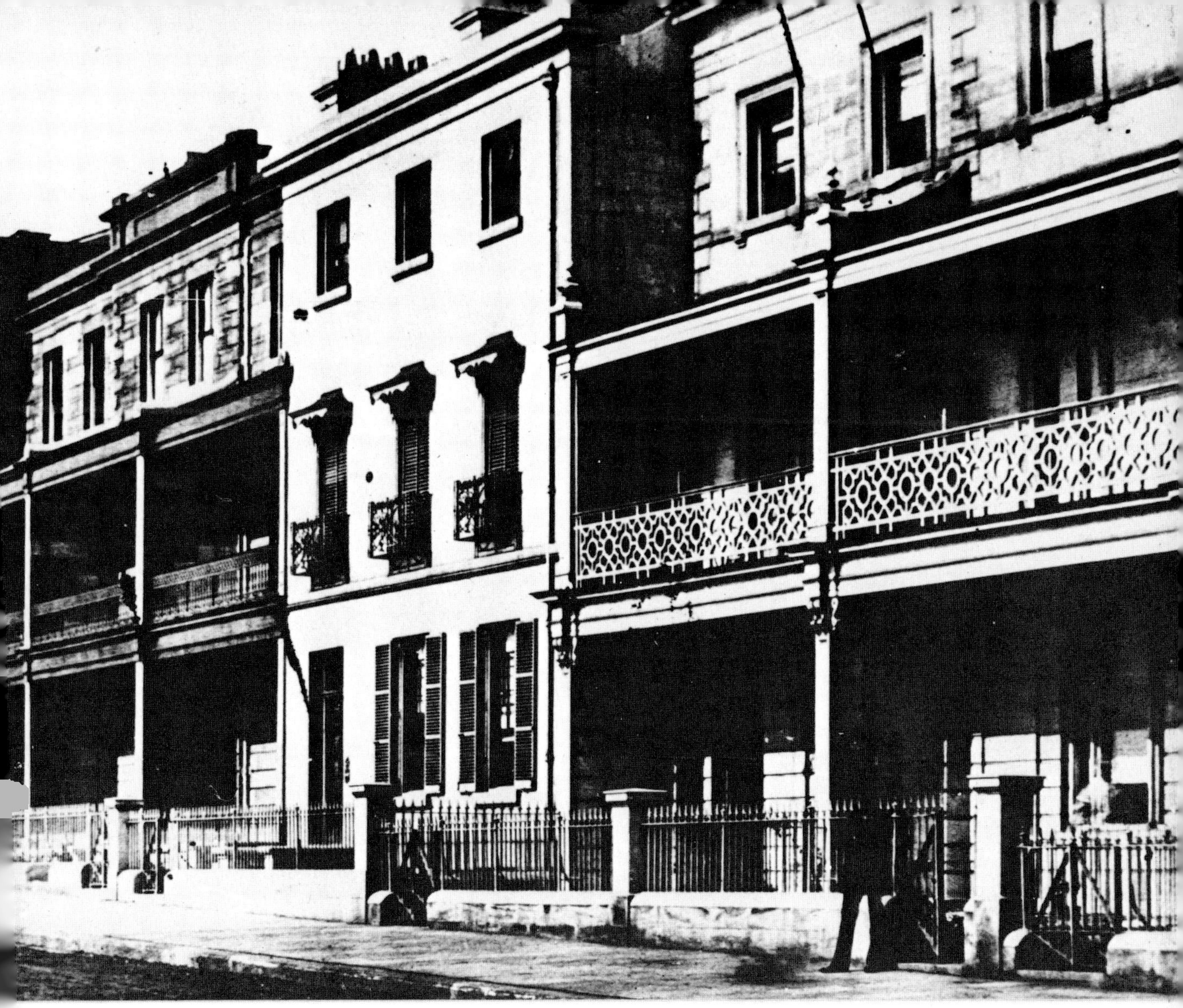

2] Houses in Macquarie Street, just north of Bent
ove Street. Taken in the 1870s by Professor John Smith of Sydney University.

13] *below* Female School of Industry, Macquarie Street, 1870. Opened in 1826 to train girls as servants, it was one of the oldest child welfare institutions in the Colony.

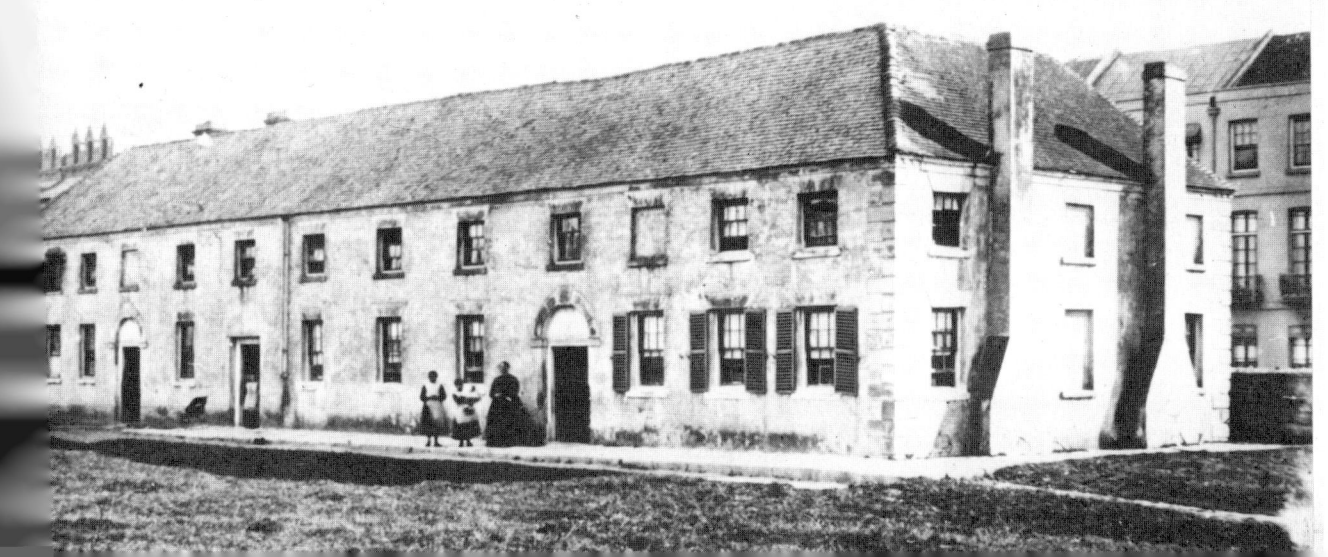

14] The Australian Museum, College Street, 1894
15] Customs House, Circular Quay, 1870
Many public buildings of the Victorian period were built of sandstone. The work of the stonemasons lent character to the growing town, later lost with the advance of steel and concrete.

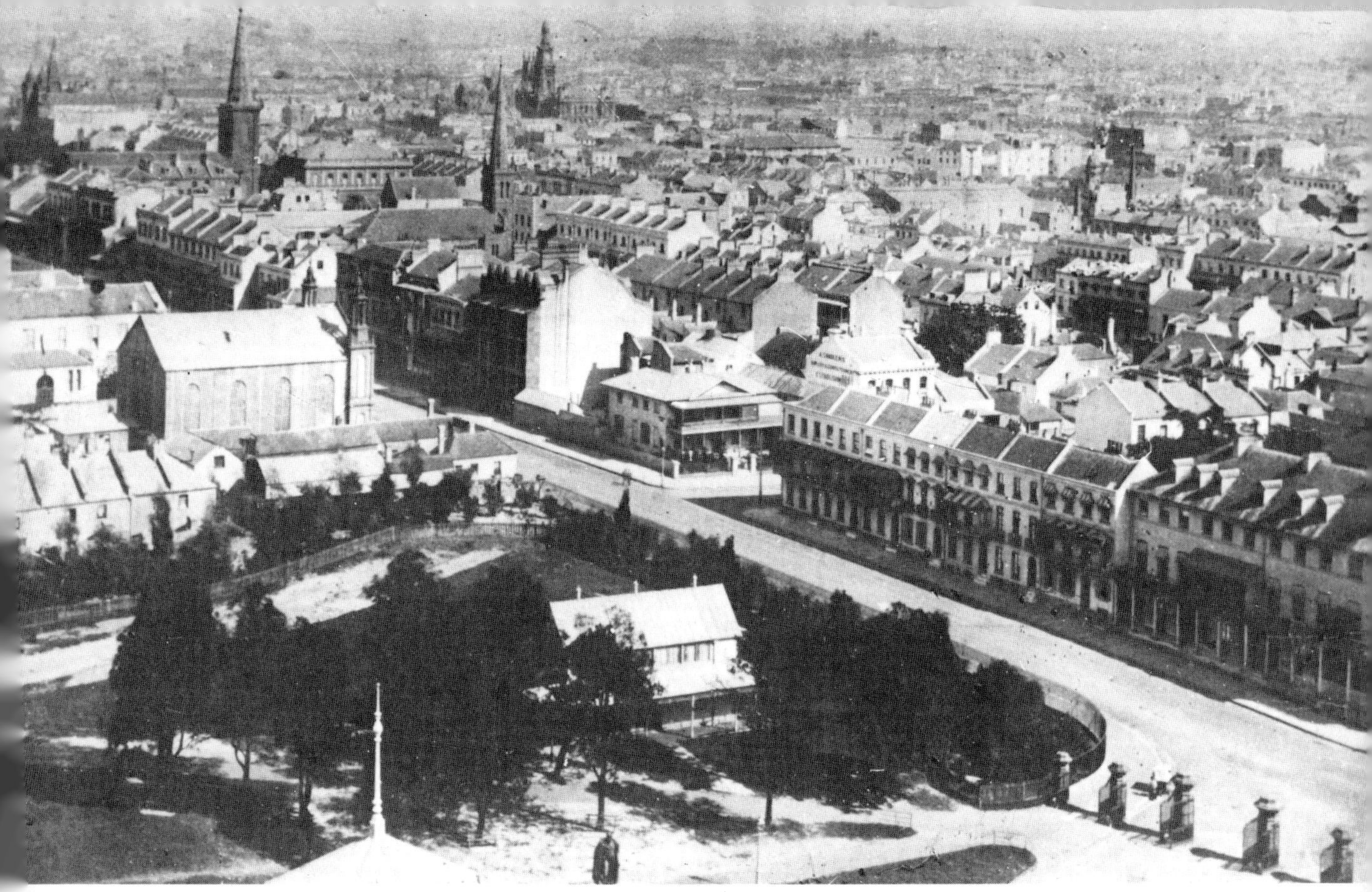

16] *above* Macquarie Street, 1880, from the roof of the Garden Palace, looking south-west towards Hunter Street. The Mitchell Library site is in the foreground.

17] *below* Wynyard Park, looking south-west from near the corner of Carrington and Margaret Streets, with a horse-bus dozing in the sun.

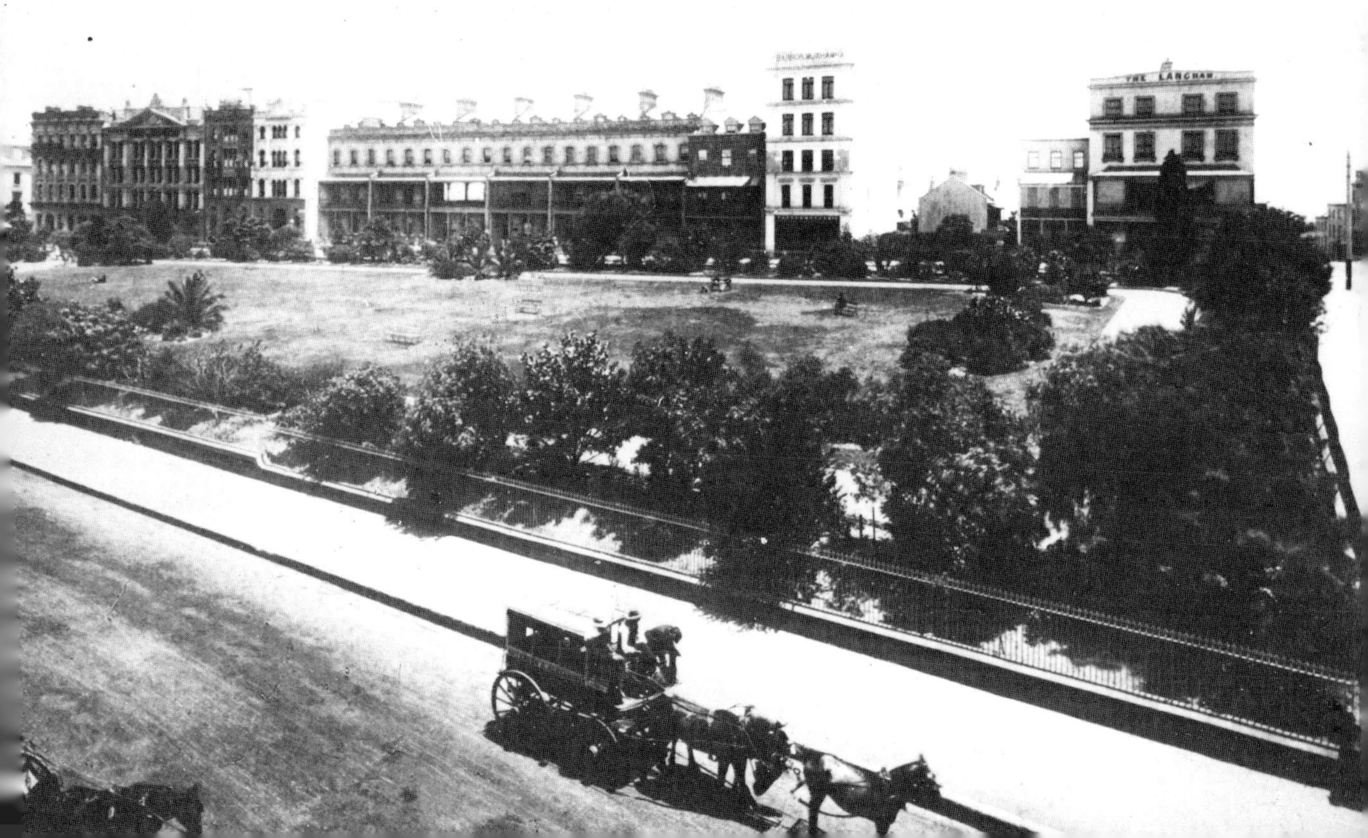

18] The Rocks Area about 1902, late afternoon. This is the right-hand part of a panoramic photograph by Charles Kerry (*the other part* is No. 7). It was taken from Observatory Hill and looks across Sydney Cove to the newly built Fort Macquarie tramway depot on Bennelong Point, beyond to Pinchgut and Bradley's Head down the Harbour. The signal flags in the foreground were used to send messages to shipping. The Rocks (given that name because of outcrops in the landscape in First Fleet times) was one of the earliest settled localities in Sydney.

For many years it had a reputation as unsavoury as the North Shore and Lane Cove. In 1858 W. S. Jevons, an Englishman working in Sydney, wrote: "I am acquainted with some of the worst parts of London, such as Jacob's Island, Golden Square, Lambeth, Derry Lane, etc., and with the most unhealthy parts of Liverpool, Paris, and other towns, but nowhere have I seen such a retreat for filth and vice as 'the Rocks'."

19] Horse-bus days in George Street, near the G.P.O. corner, in the 1890s, looking across to David Jones on the corner of Barrack Street. Horse-drawn omnibuses, like the one in the photograph, were on regular routes to the suburbs. In December 1899 electric tram services ran through the heart of the city for the first time, with the opening of the line from Circular Quay to Pyrmont. Taken by Henry King.

20] In the banking chamber of the Bank of New South Wales, 341 George Street, about 1904.

Two views of George Street in 1910

21] *top* The G.P.O. corner at Martin Place, looking south. The paper-seller has a poster for the *Evening News*, a popular newspaper of the times.

22] *bottom* A white-helmeted policeman directs traffic as a crowded Circular Quay tram pulls up at the King Street stop.

23] The General Post Office, George Street, before
above Martin Place was created. Thompson & Giles advertised themselves as "The Busy Drapers".

24] George Street, looking towards King Street, 187
below It could have been early Sunday morning when th
photograph was taken.

25] Martin Place, 1900, before it was extended from Phillip Street to Macquarie Street, and before the building of Challis House. It was created partly from acquired land and a narrow thoroughfare known variously as "Post Office Place", "Post Office Street", and "St. Martin's Lane" between George and Pitt Streets; "Foxlow Place" and Moore Street between Pitt and Castlereagh Streets. It was probably named after Irish-born Sir James Martin (1820-86), journalist, essayist, politician (Premier several times), and finally, Chief Justice of New South Wales.

26] "O listen to the band!" in Hyde Park, not far from the Australian Museum. Yesterday's Sydneysiders found it a pleasant Sunday afternoon social occasion, while the uniformed musicians played popular melodies from the rotunda.

Governor Lachlan Macquarie in a Government and General Order 6th October, 1810, created and named Hyde Park from unoccupied ground "for the Recreation and Amusement of the Inhabitants of the Town, and as a Field of Exercise for the Troops."

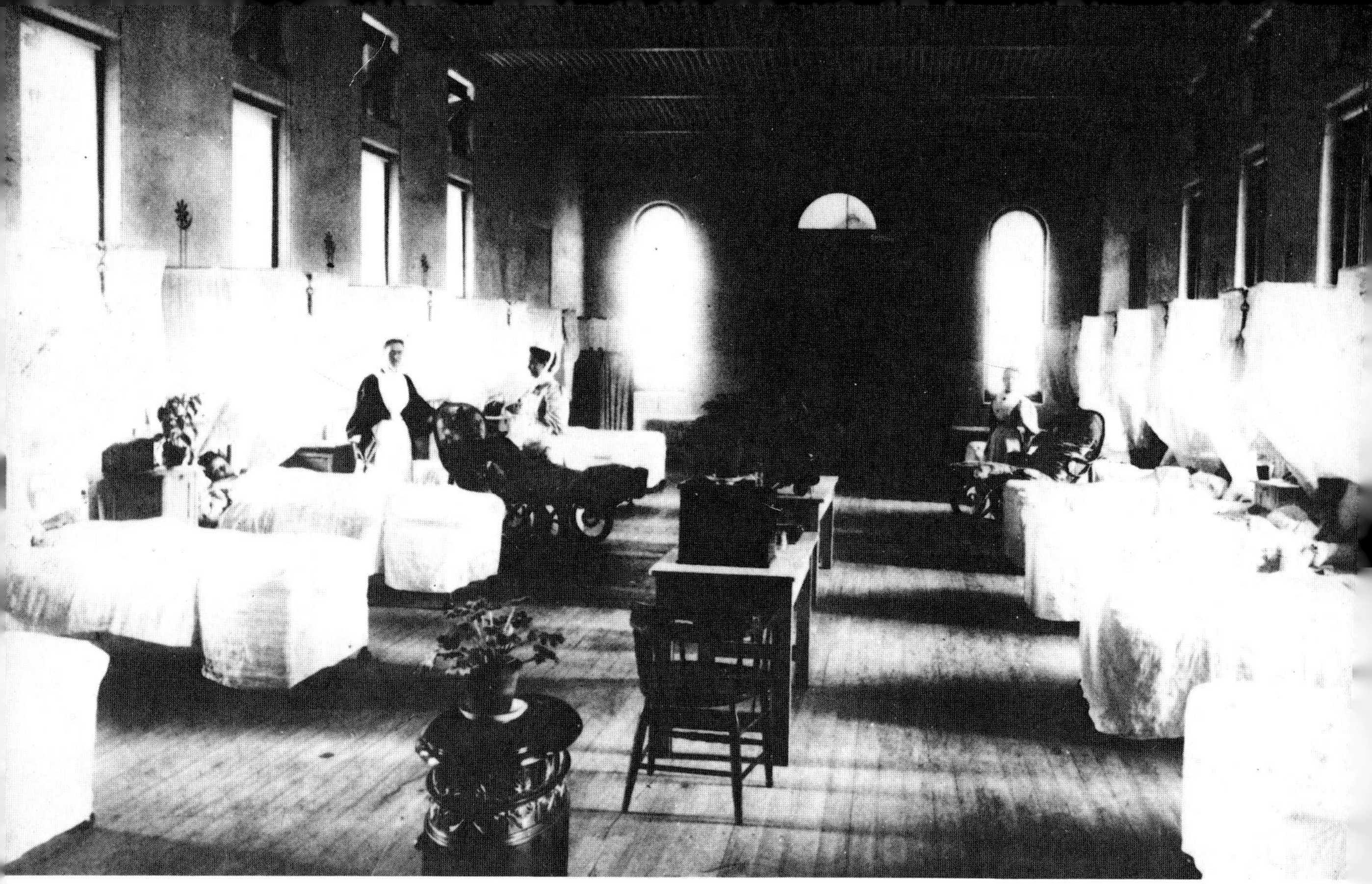

27] *above* A ward in Sydney Hospital in the 1890s. The present hospital was created by Act of Parliament in 1881, and a new building opened in 1894.

28] *below* Sydney Infirmary and Dispensary, Macquarie Street on the site of Sydney Hospital. Founded 1826. All that remains is the North Wing, now State Parliament House.

29] George Street, 1894, looking south across the King Street intersection. Carts, wagons, and horse-buses and hansom cabs clip-clopped and swayed in leisurely fashion through the city; and those who walked didn't seem to hurry either.

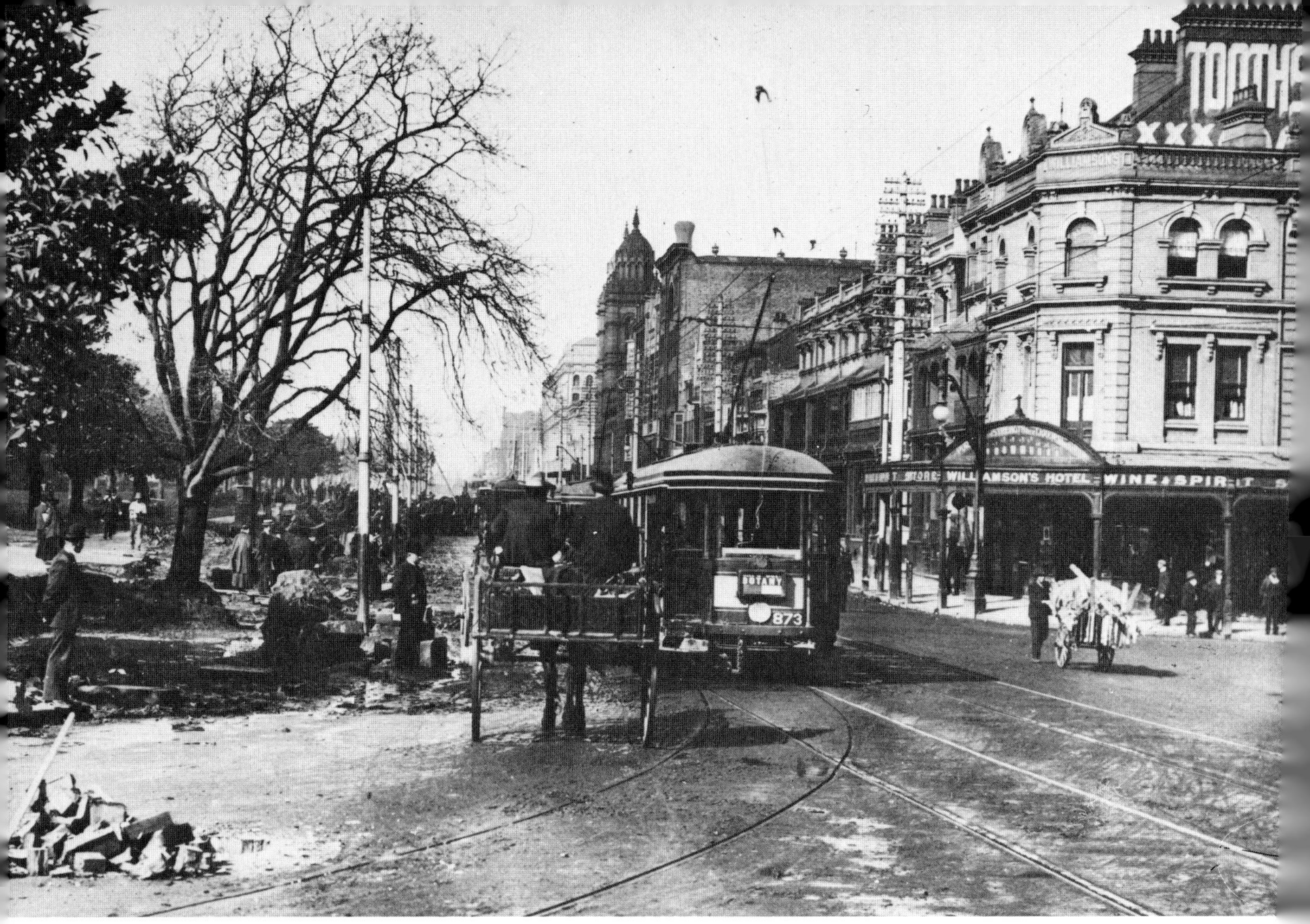
TOOTHS
XXX
WILLIAMSON'S
WILLIAMSON'S HOTEL
WINE & SPIR
BOTANY
873

30]

31]

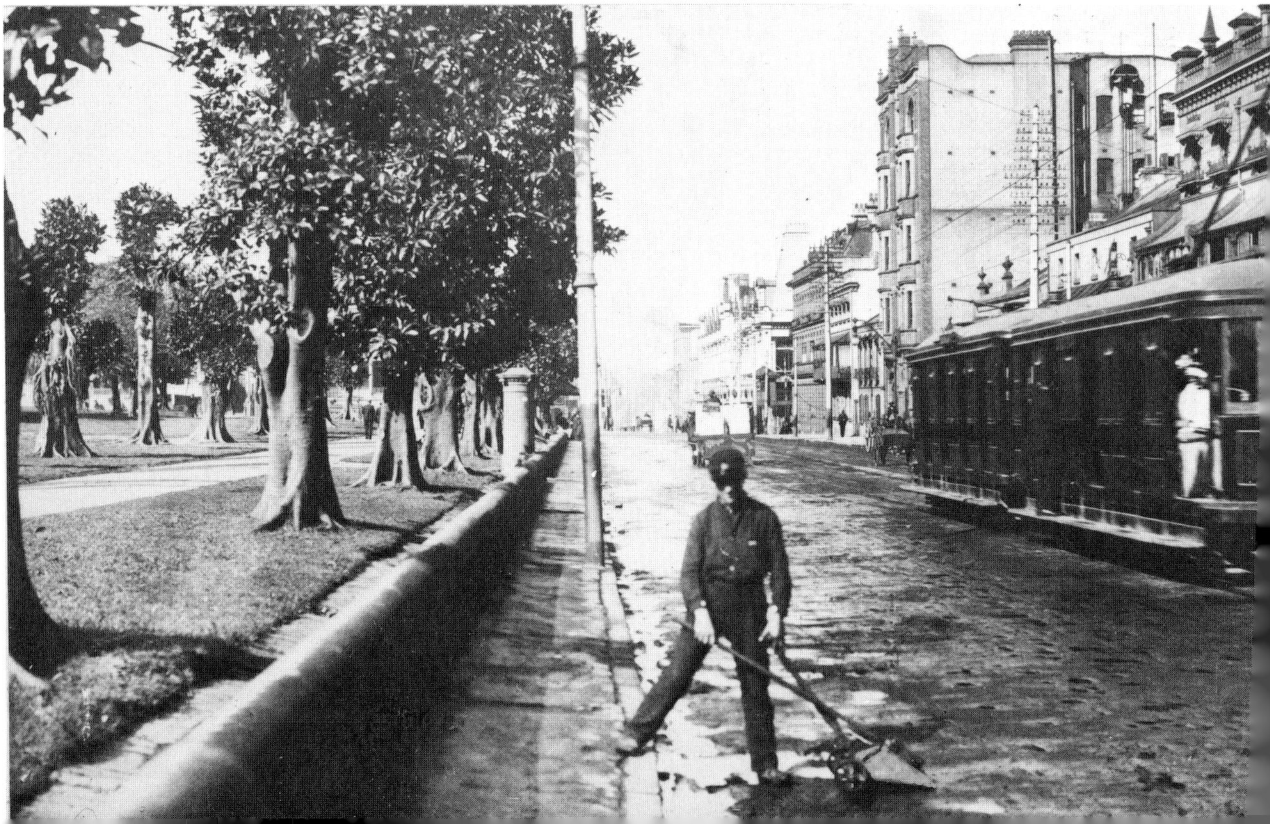

The City Council widens Elizabeth Street, 1909. Taken near St. James Road and Market Street, looking south towards the Great Synagogue.

31] Elizabeth Street, 1909, looking south from Bathurst Street. In the foreground is a "sparrow-starver" or "block boy", the City Council street-sweeper responsible for a city block.

32] *above* A row of trees felled to widen Elizabeth Street in 1909. City Council outdoor staff work with pick and shovel and crowbar, while a horse and dray waits to take material away. Taken from near Park Street, with the spire of St. James' Church in the distance at right.

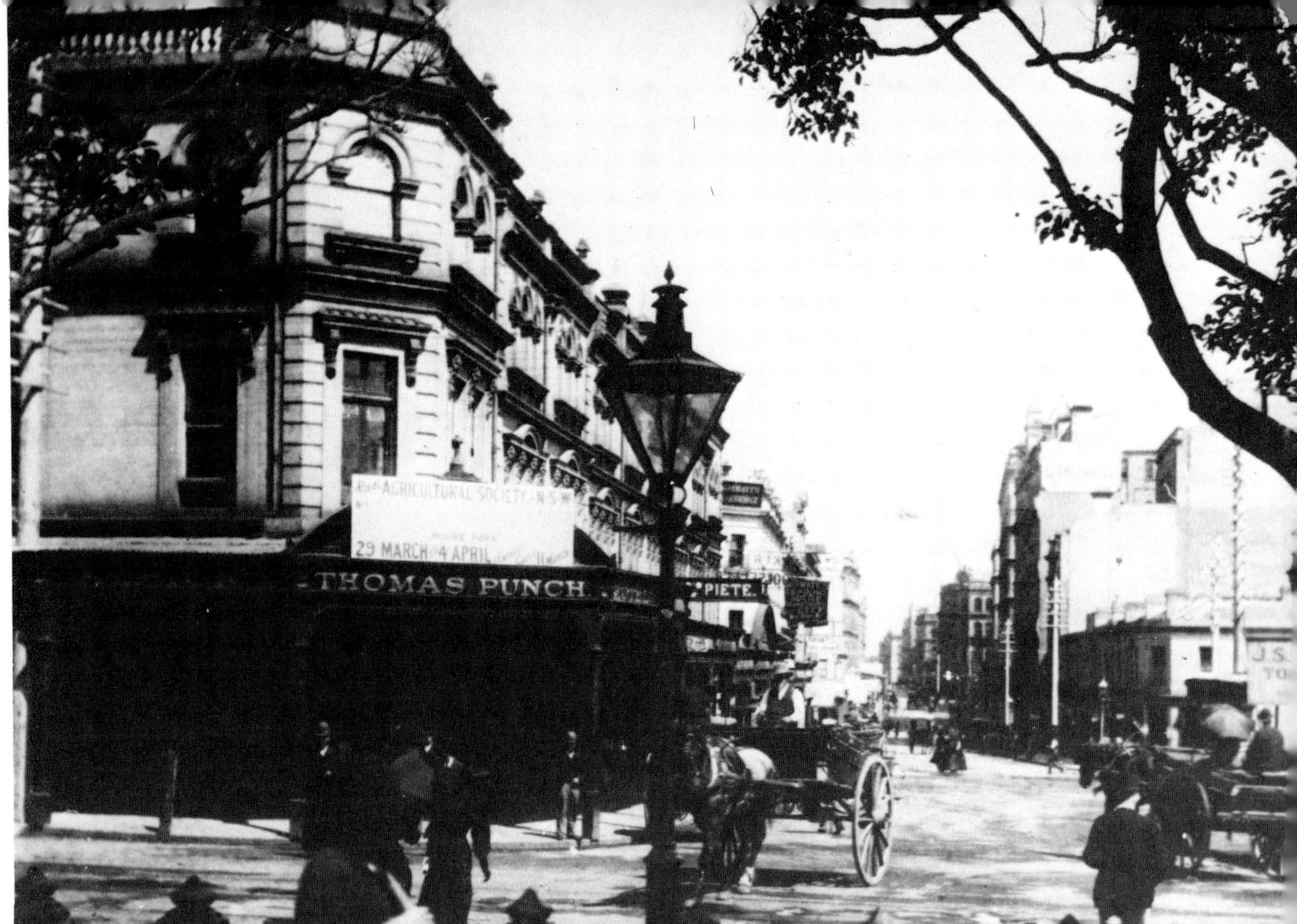
AGRICULTURAL SOCIETY N.S.W.
29 MARCH 4 APRIL
THOMAS PUNCH
PIETE

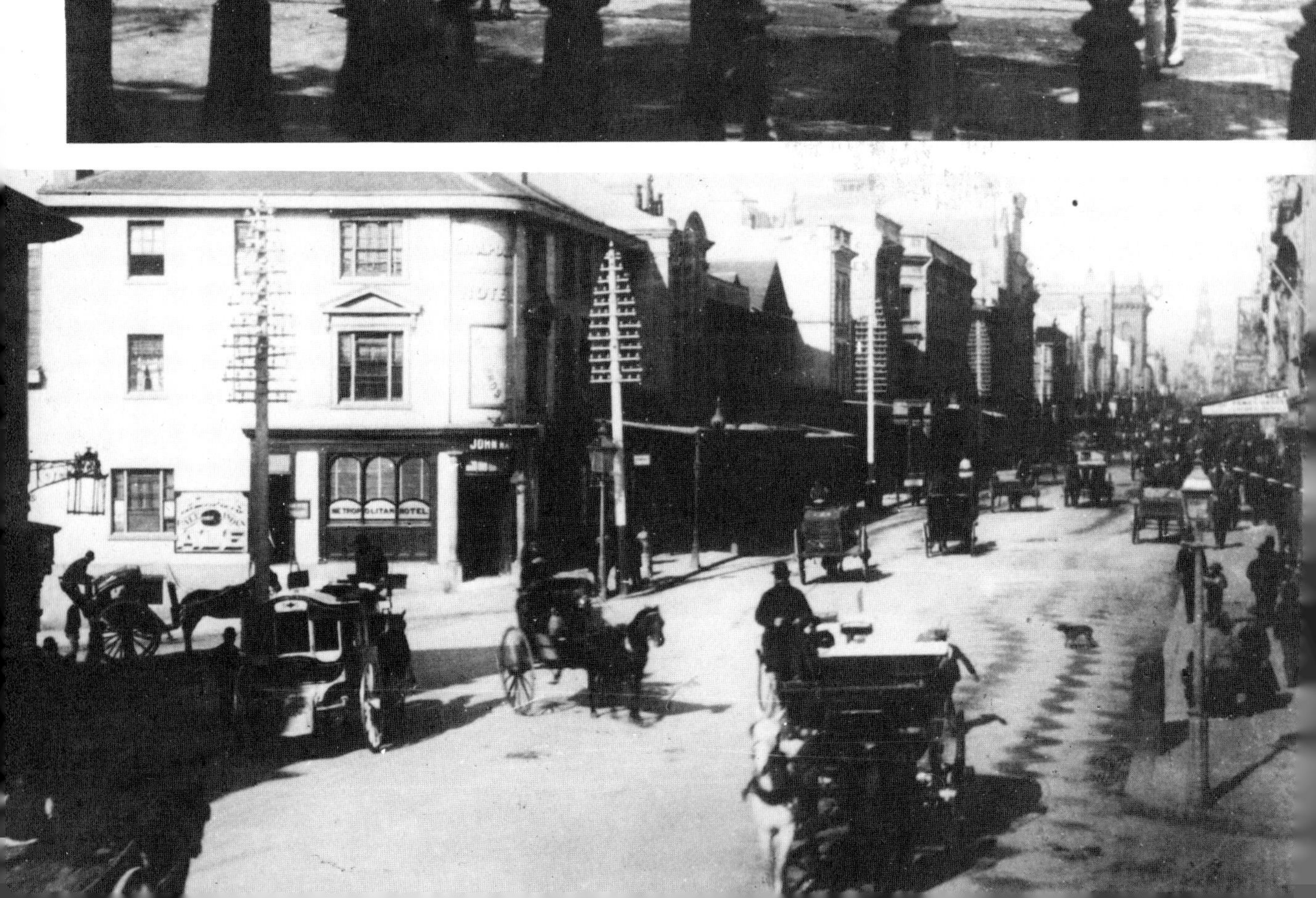
METROPOLITAN HOTEL

33] Market Street, 1893, looking towards George Street from Hyde Park on the opposite side of Elizabeth Street. Steam trams began running along Elizabeth Street from Redfern Station to Hunter Street terminus in 1879.

top left

34] George Street, near Bridge Street, about 1890. All the traffic is horse drawn, and typical of the footpath scene are gas street-lamps, hitching posts, and telegraph poles, some carrying a dozen cross-arms.

bottom left

35] Pitt Street, looking north from the Market Street intersection, about 1890. A privately owned horse-tram service ran up Pitt Street in the 1860s, but was removed by Act of Parliament because people objected to the type of imported rails used, which stood above the surface of the roadway.

above

36] Queen Victoria Markets, George Street, about 1900

37] George Street, looking towards the Haymarket, in the 1890s

38] Traffic from the city coming off Pyrmont Bridge, 1910. There were then 2551 motor-cars registered in New South Wales; in 1911 there were 3992, and in 1912, 5985.

39] *below* The original Pyrmont Bridge, a privately-owned wooden structure opened in 1859. Tolls were charged: carriages, 9d.; horses, 3d.; sheep, one farthing; oxen, one penny; horses, twopence.

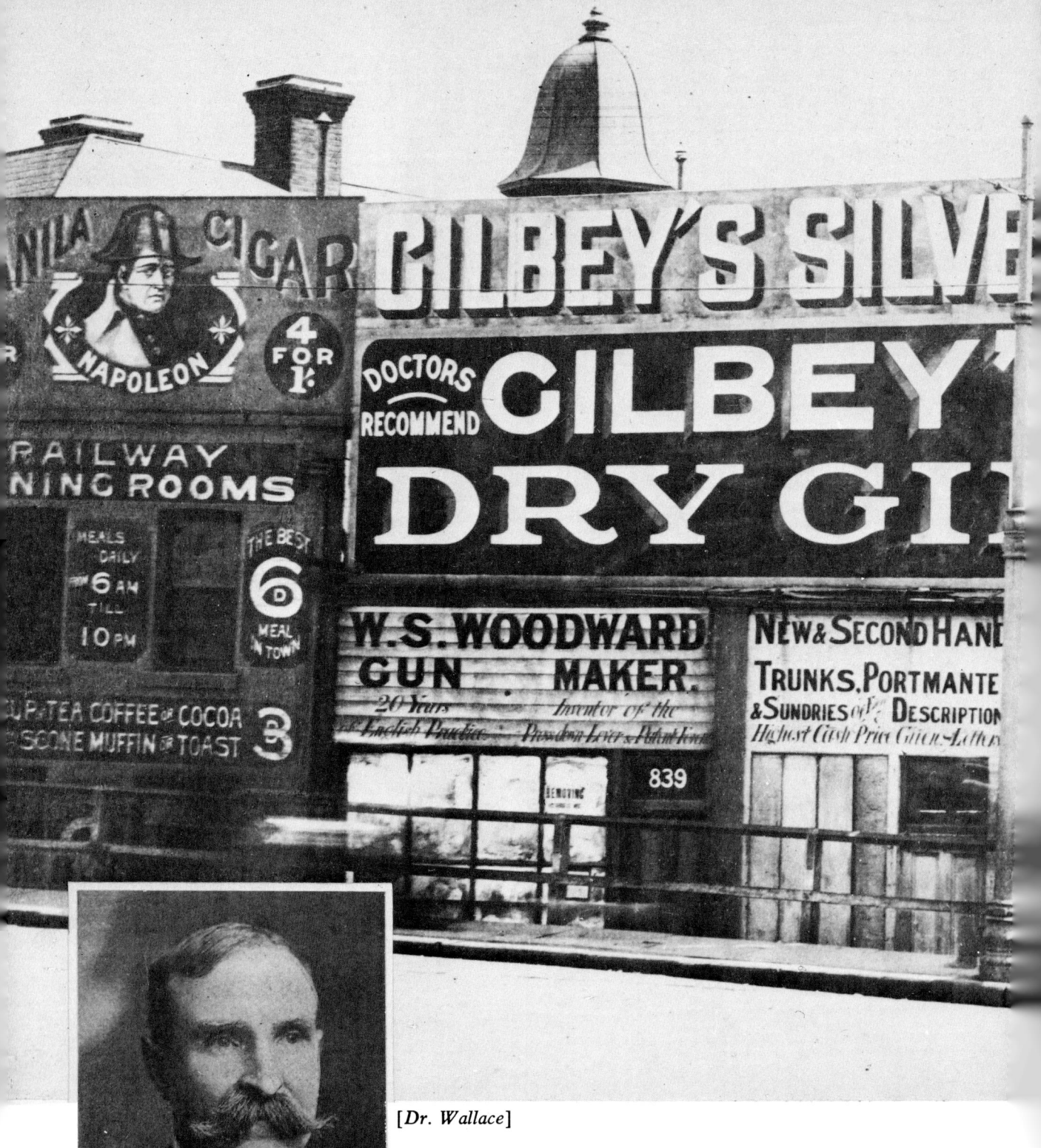

[Dr. Wallace]

40] Hoardings on Nos. 835-841 George Street, near Harris Street, about 1900. Freeman and Wallace were among those members of the medical profession who bought advertising space in the Press. From the *Town & Country Journal*, 9th March 1901: "Howard Freeman, Sydney's Leading Specialist. Professor of Electricity, Dr. Harmon's

[Dr. Freeman]

College, Washington Cor., Cal., U.S.A. Richard Wallace, M.D., L.R.C.P., L.F.P.S., Late Medical Staff, British Army, Late Consulting Staff, Homoepathic Hospital, Melbourne." They claimed to have the largest practice in Australia.

41] The reading room of the library of the Sydney
above School of Arts in Pitt Street in the 1890s.

42] A horse-bus passes the Central Police Office, on the
below west side of George Street between Market and
Druitt Streets. The building was designed by Francis
Greenway for use as a Market House.

43]
above

At the turn of the century tobacco was still something to be enjoyed. Women might complain about it making the curtains smell, but manufacturers could boast of their sales with a clear conscience. The worst was to come. Part of the income from tobacco shares was some fifty years later used to create the Dixson Gallery of Australian art and the Dixson Library in the Library of New South Wales.

44]
below

Inhabitants of the Rocks come out for a sticky-beak at the camera. A scene not far from the Whaler's Arms.

45] **George Street**, looking south from Bathurst Street
above **down to Brickfield Hill and Railway Square.** In those horse-drawn days there was no parking problem.

46] King Street at the George Street intersection, looking
below to Elizabeth Street, 1890s. Cable trams to Edgecliff began running in King Street in 1894.

47]
top

A white cat, a black cat, and a little girl catch the sun on the front steps of the Friends' Meeting House. Built in 1868, it was demolished to make way for Central Railway Station.

48]
bottom

The Benevolent Asylum, Pitt Street, opposite Christ Church St. Lawrence, now part of Central Station. The foundation stone read: "This Asylum for the Poor, Blind, Aged, and Infirm was erected in 1820, L. Macquarie, Esq., being Governor". Administered by the Benevolent Society with government and private support it provided for about 60 persons.

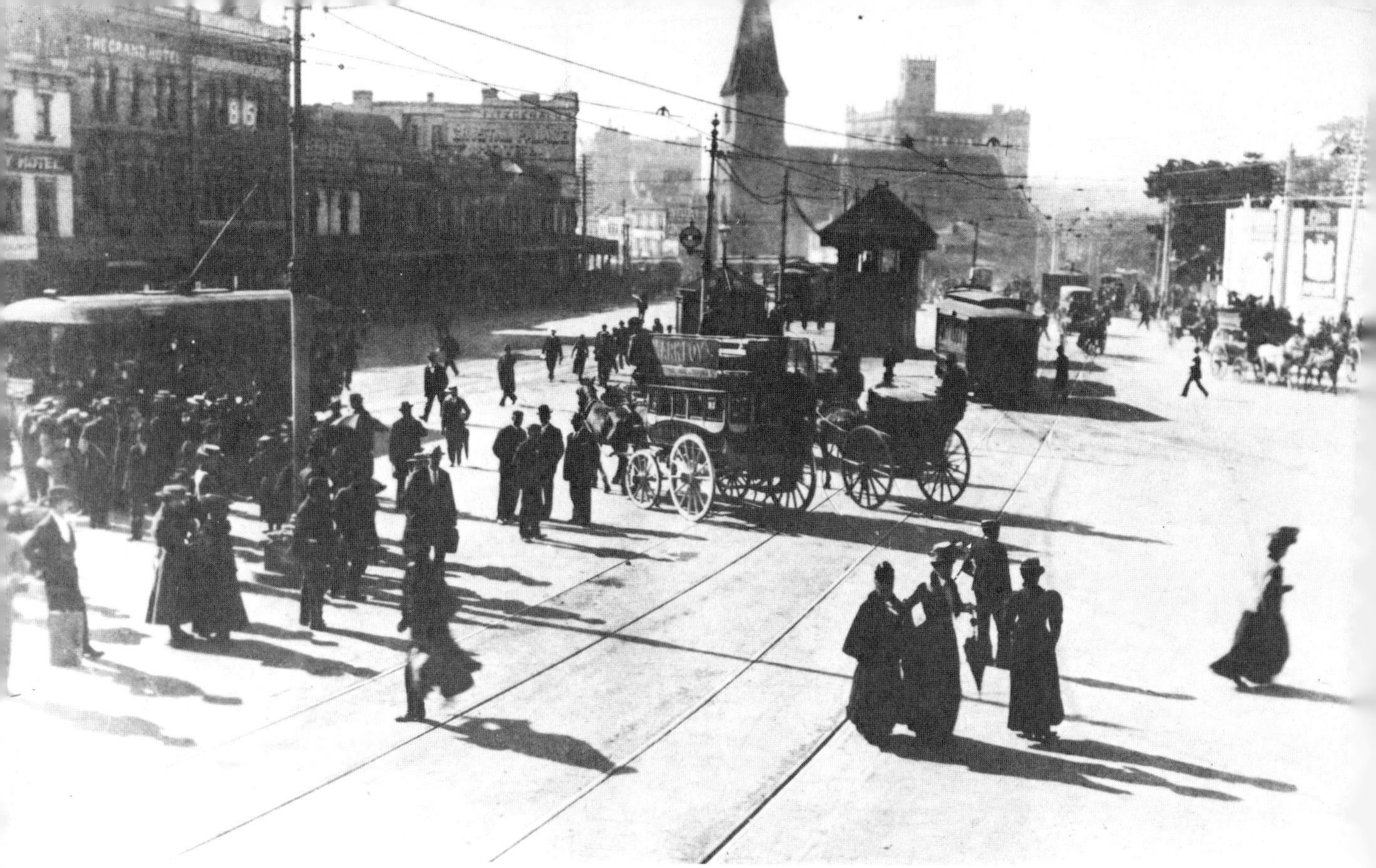

49] Waiting for trams in Railway Square, about the turn
above of the century. A horse-bus and a hansom cab stand
with impunity across the tram tracks; pedestrian
crossings are a thing of the future.

50] Redfern Station, chief Sydney railway terminus be-
below fore Central was built. The first steam-tram service,
from Hunter Street via Elizabeth Street, terminated
here in 1879.

51] The tramway section at Sydney Railway Gates (now Railway Square) in 1908; always a busy place, with travellers waiting to catch trams to the various Western Suburbs or to Circular Quay. The Premier (Charles Gregory Wade) likened it to the neck of a bottle through which thousands passed daily. Although the city's extensive system of electric tramways was regarded as among the best public transport systems in the world, the need for more suburban railways had become obvious even before the first World War.

OUT IN THE SUBURBS

52] *above*
On the verandah of Drummoyne House, Wright's Point, overlooking the Parramatta River, probably in the 1860s. The man could be William Wright, who built the house in the 1850s.

53] *above right*
Professor John Smith makes a time exposure on the verandah of Drummoyne House. He is wearing his usual stove-pipe hat.

54] *below right*
An interior photograph taken at Drummoyne House. The three attractive sisters are said to be the daughters of Spencer Bayley, of Hunter's Hill, close friend of William Wright.

55] *above* Drummoyne House, taken probably in the 1860s, a photograph by Professor John Smith. William Wright, who built it, was an Islands trader who came to Sydney in 1838, and is said to have made his money on expeditions to New Zealand in the 1840s.

56] *below* "Strathmore", Glebe, home of George Wigram Allen (1824-1885), early solicitor and politician, and for many years a trustee of Sydney Grammar School.

57] New Canterbury Road, Petersham, in 1914.

58] New Canterbury Road, Dulwich Hill, 1914, junction of the Dulwich Hill to Addison Road, and Petersham to Hurlstone Park tramways.

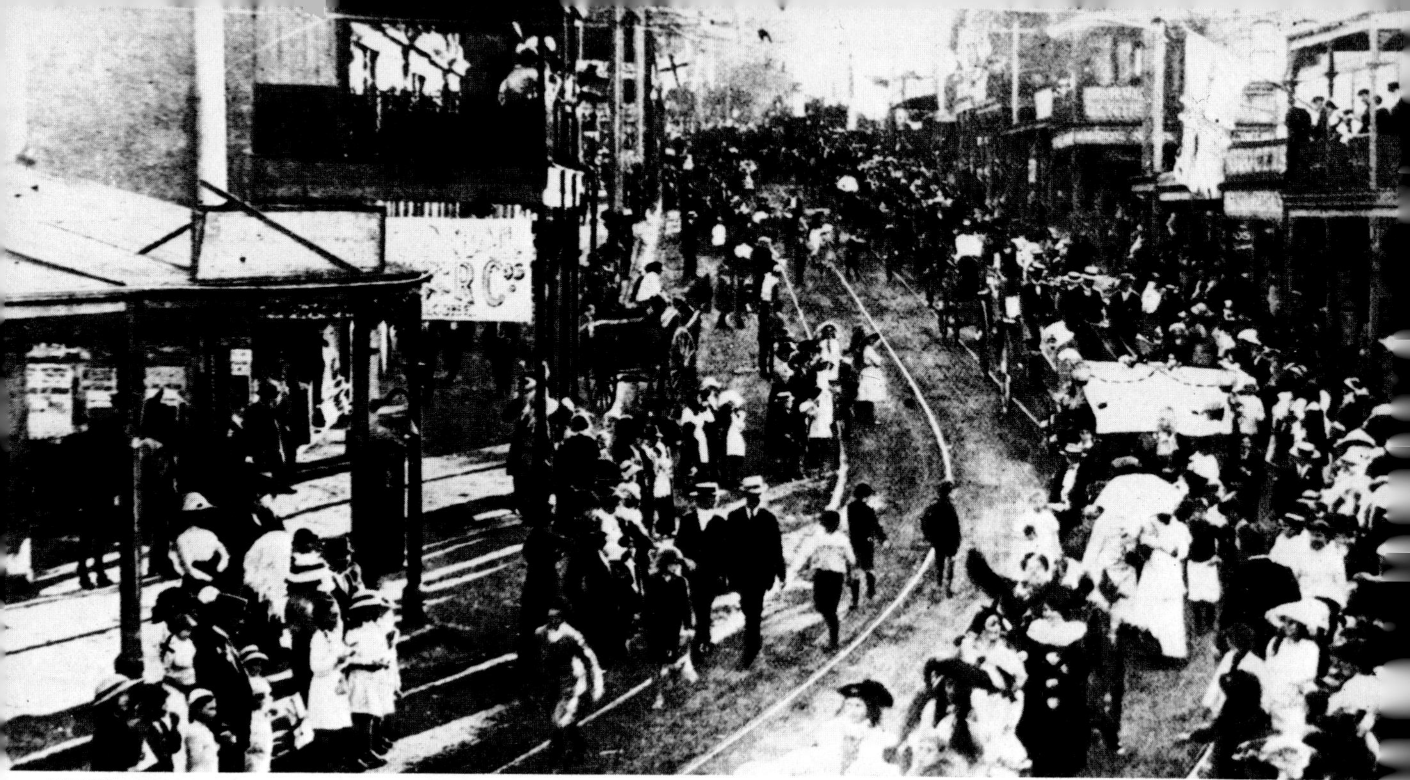

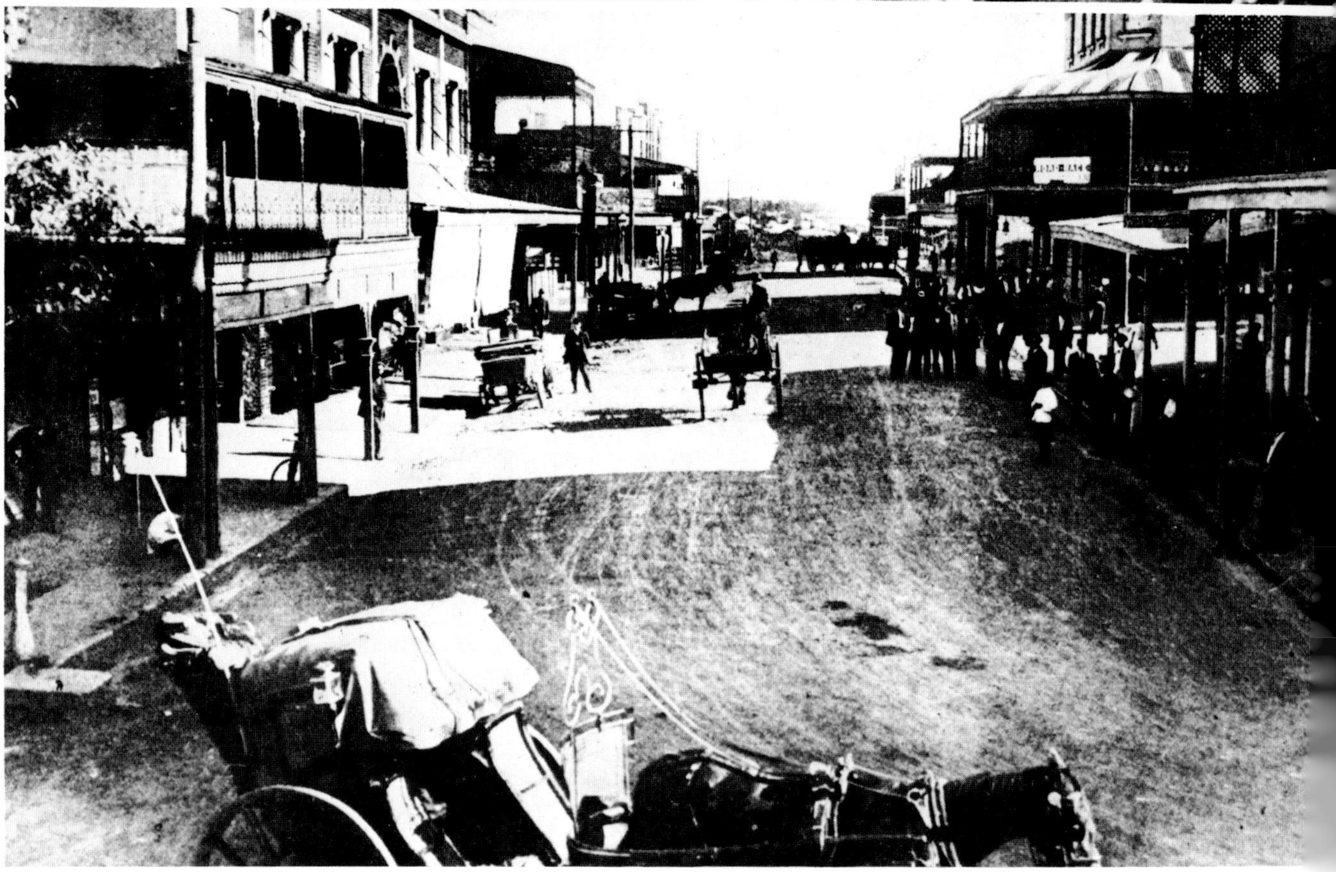

59] Monster procession of the Balmain & Rozelle Carnival, 1914.
top

60] South Street, Granville, in 1914.
bottom

61] Vehicle ferry, Middle Harbour, opposite The Spit, 1890s.

62] Waiting for the punt, Tom Ugly's Point.

63] Woolloomooloo Bay in the 1860s, looking from the Domain towards the heights of King's Cross. Taken by Professor John Smith.

64] Victoria Barracks, Paddington, 1871. Taken from near Oatley Road. Oxford Street is at the left.

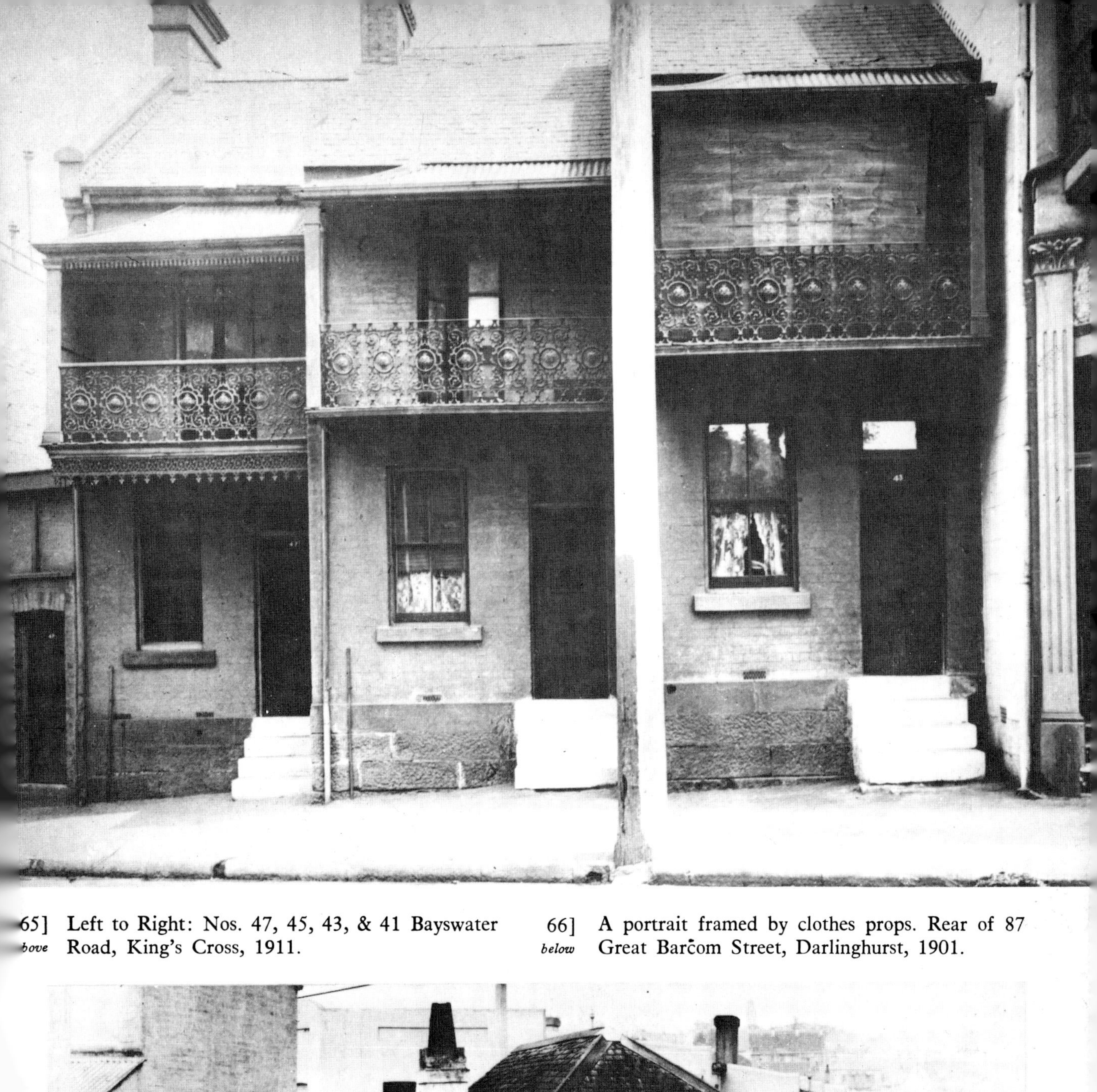

65] *above* Left to Right: Nos. 47, 45, 43, & 41 Bayswater Road, King's Cross, 1911.

66] *below* A portrait framed by clothes props. Rear of 87 Great Barcom Street, Darlinghurst, 1901.

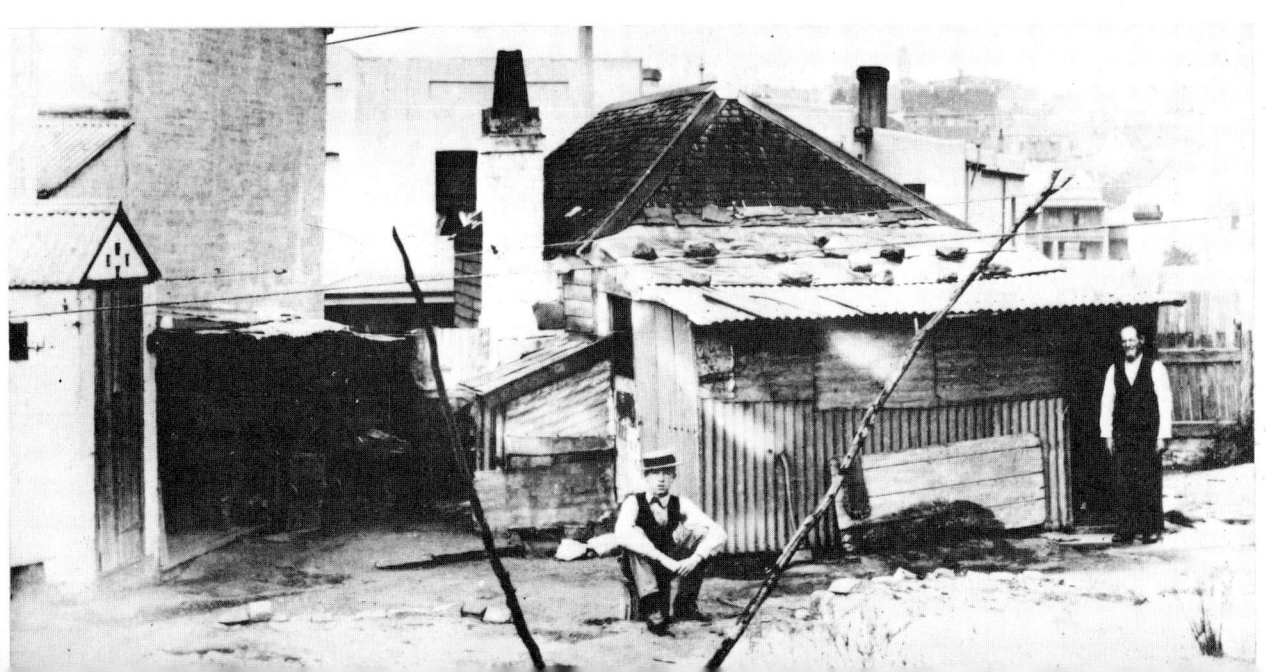

67] Coogee Beach in the 1890s.   68] Bondi Beach, about 1894.

69] The Old and the New at South Head, 1883. At left is the first lighthouse built in Australia. It was erected by order of Governor Macquarie in 1817, designed by Francis Greenway, and was called the Macquarie Light. It was said to have been visible at night for 24 miles. Demolished.

At the Beach, 1914

top left 70] Manly Lifesaving Club's lookout tower.

above 71] Bondi lifesavers bring a "patient" ashore.

left 72] Mum and the kids get their feet wet.

below 73] Coogee lifesavers run out with the line.

74] Spit Junction, Mosman, 1914, in the heydey of the pedestrian.

75] Alfred Street, North Sydney. The cable tram service from Milson's Point to Ridge Street began in 1886.

76] Looking down the Lane Cove River as the ferry steams towards Sydney, with old Fig Tree Bridge in the foreground.

77] Greenwich Point Wharf before the first World War.

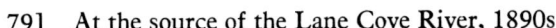

78] A picnic up the Lane Cove River. Professor Smith, at right, with stove-pipe hat, probably took the photograph.

79] At the source of the Lane Cove River, 1890s.

80] Ernest Leafe's general store, Penshurst Street, Willoughby, built in 1885. It served also as a postal and money order office, and a savings bank.

81] Willoughby Council displays its new road-making equipment in Victoria Avenue, Chatswood, about 1913.

82] The Corso, Manly, before the first World War. A steam-tram service began running from Manly to Curl Curl in 1903.

83] Manly's Ocean Beach, in the days when the pines were young and neck-to-knee was the fashion.

84] 'The Village", as Manly was called in 1913, was already "an important Sydney watering-place", where visitors often spent their summer vacation.

85] In the surf at Manly, 1913. Mothers then believed firmly that children should protect their skin from the sun, and dressed them accordingly.

EMPORIUMS AND SHOPS

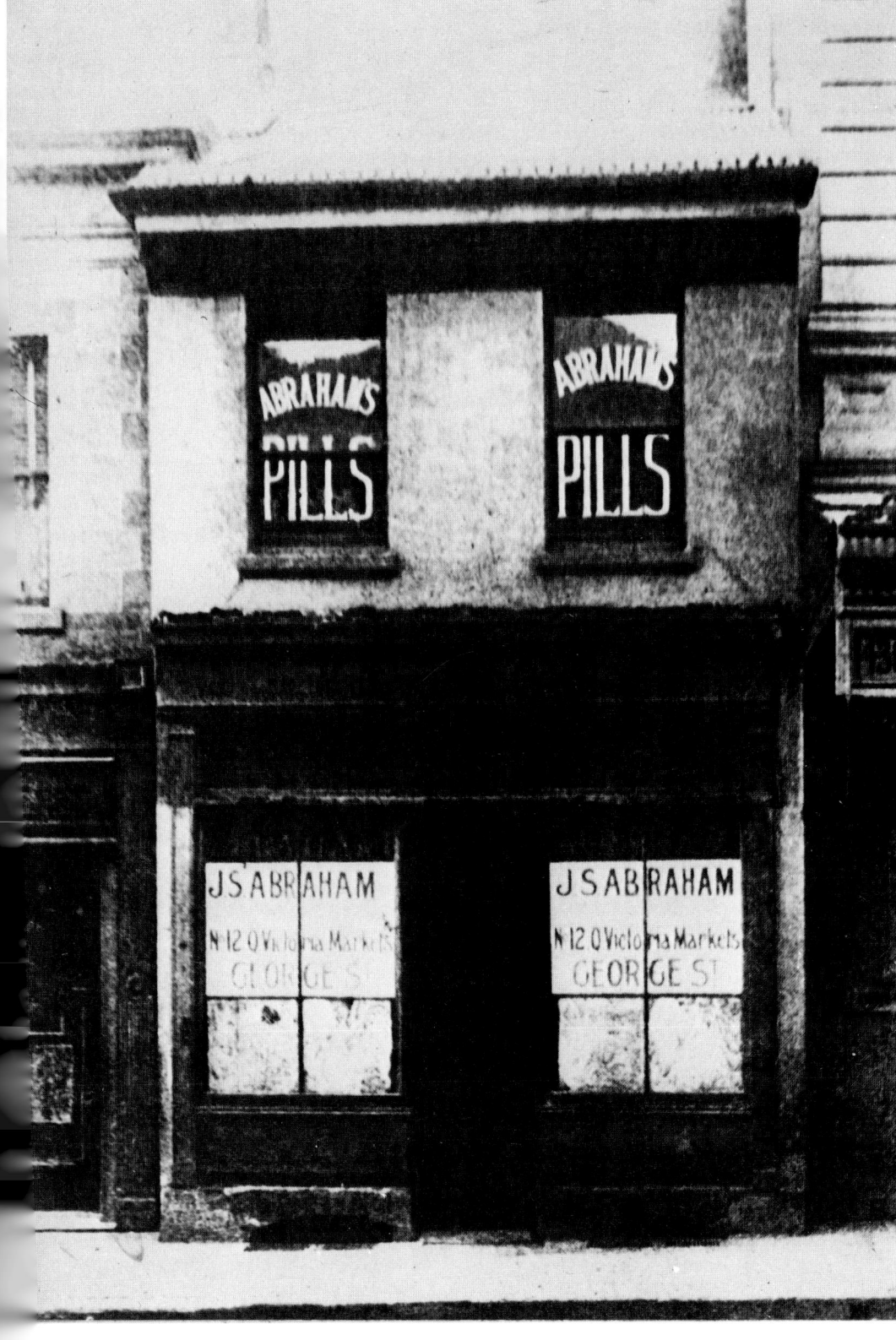

86] J. S. Abraham's chemist's shop, 434 George Street, 1901. An old landmark, it stood out nearly three feet beyond adjoining buildings. Abraham's father began there as Chemist and Druggist in the 1840s. Later he sold quicksilver to miners who believed it had an affinity with gold.

87] Marcus Clark (1859-1913) came to Australia in the 1880s. He first worked at Newtown, and in 1883 opened on his own account in a little single-fronted shop with six assistants. In 1896 he opened a branch at North Sydney, the first of many in the State. In 1905 he bought from the N.S.W. Government, land at the corner of Pitt and George Streets, where he erected the eight-storey department store shown here. Another big store was built in Railway Square.

88] Mrs. Annie Whitehead's "Federal Fruit Mart", 92 Cleveland Street and Harkness Lane, Chippendale, in 1907. Next door, Mrs. Annie Pincham conducted a fish shop, while No. 96 was occupied by Thomas Coady, who described himself as a horse-dealer.

89] W. A. Grubb's butchery, 149 George Street, 1913, when new premises were opened. Stock were then taken from Flemington saleyards to the grazing paddocks and abattoir at Botany. Mr. Grubb came to Australia in the 1880s from Scotland. He died in Sydney in 1914. The business flourishes still.

90] The genesis of Farmer & Co.: one of these small shops in Pitt Street, near Market
above Street, where Joseph Farmer began business in 1840. His original premises were 24 feet frontage and 75 feet deep. In 1873 they were demolished to build the "Victoria House" store.

91] Farmer's "New Show-Room, Specially Devoted to the Display of French and British
below Silks, Mantles, Jackets, and Evening Dresses" in the 1870s.

92] *above left*   John Pope (1827-1912), who became a partner in Farmer's in 1869, and expanded the business considerably.

93] *above right*   Joseph Farmer (1813-1890), founder of Farmer & Co., who first offered his "well selected and fashionable stock of drapery goods" to Sydney in 1840.

94] *below*   Farmer's "Victoria House", Pitt Street, designed by J. Horbury Hunt and built of red brick. This elegant store opened in 1874, but was pulled down in 1906 to make way for a larger building.

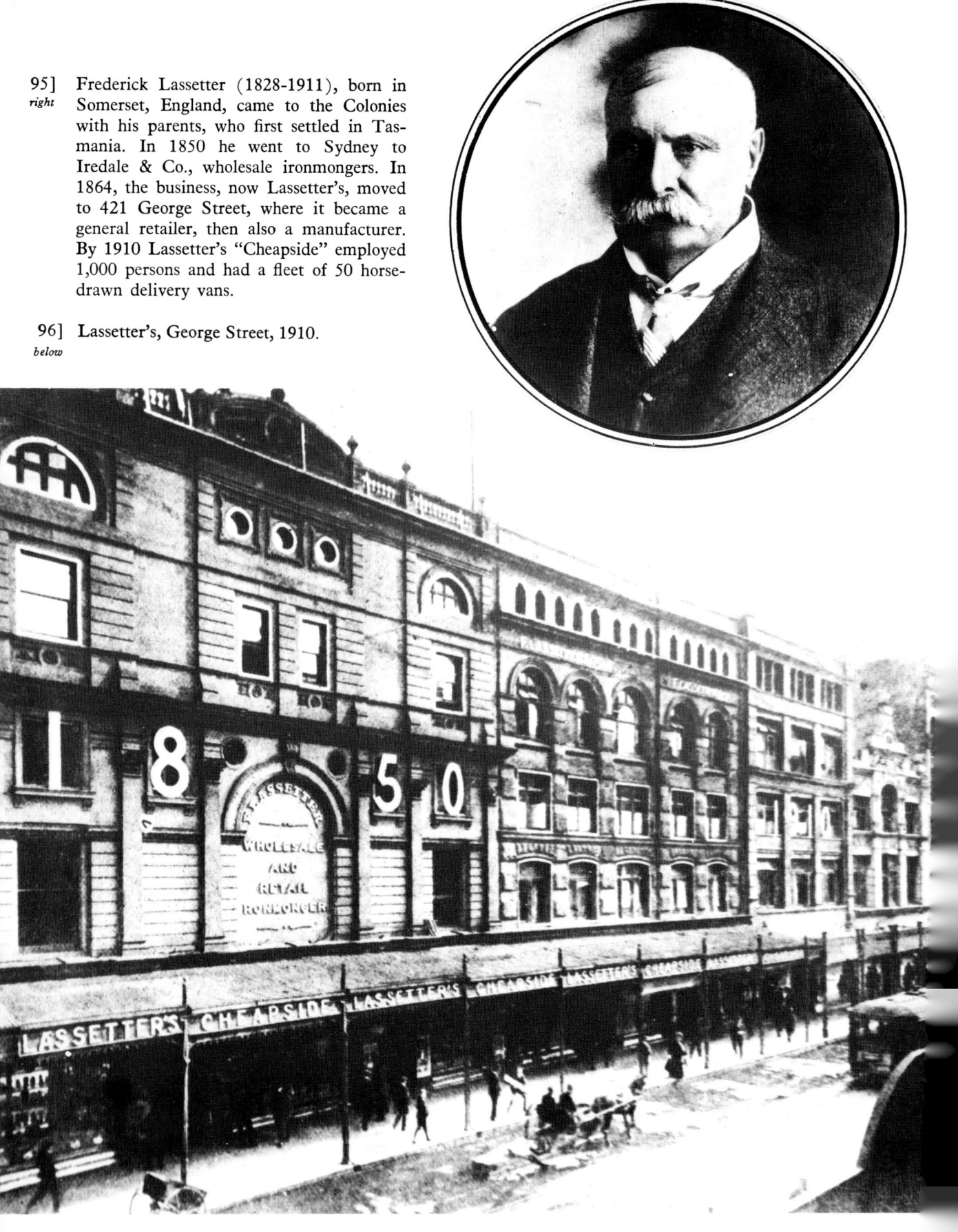

95] *right* Frederick Lassetter (1828-1911), born in Somerset, England, came to the Colonies with his parents, who first settled in Tasmania. In 1850 he went to Sydney to Iredale & Co., wholesale ironmongers. In 1864, the business, now Lassetter's, moved to 421 George Street, where it became a general retailer, then also a manufacturer. By 1910 Lassetter's "Cheapside" employed 1,000 persons and had a fleet of 50 horse-drawn delivery vans.

96] *below* Lassetter's, George Street, 1910.

97] David Jones (1793-1873), pioneer retailer, born near Llandilo, Wales, was a grocer's apprentice at fourteen. After extensive London experience he opened a shop in Sydney in 1838. He was senior deacon of the Pitt Street Congregational Church, and in 1856 was appointed to the Legislative Council.

98] David Jones & Co., George Street, about 1860 (Barrack Street is at right). The founder of the business came to this site originally after being in partnership with Charles Appleton. On 24th May 1838, he advertised in the *Sydney Morning Herald* that "having dissolved partnership with Mr. Appleton he has removed his business to those large and commodious premises opposite the General Post Office in George Street, where he will receive for the current year his usual

consignments of goods from England, and where from the highly respectable connections he has formed, he will be able to supply his correspondents upon more advantageous terms than heretofore. He also avails himself of this opportunity to return his most grateful thanks for the unparalleled support he has hitherto received, and begs to solicit a continuance of public patronage." The first shop was about 25 by 16 feet, with a room at the back.

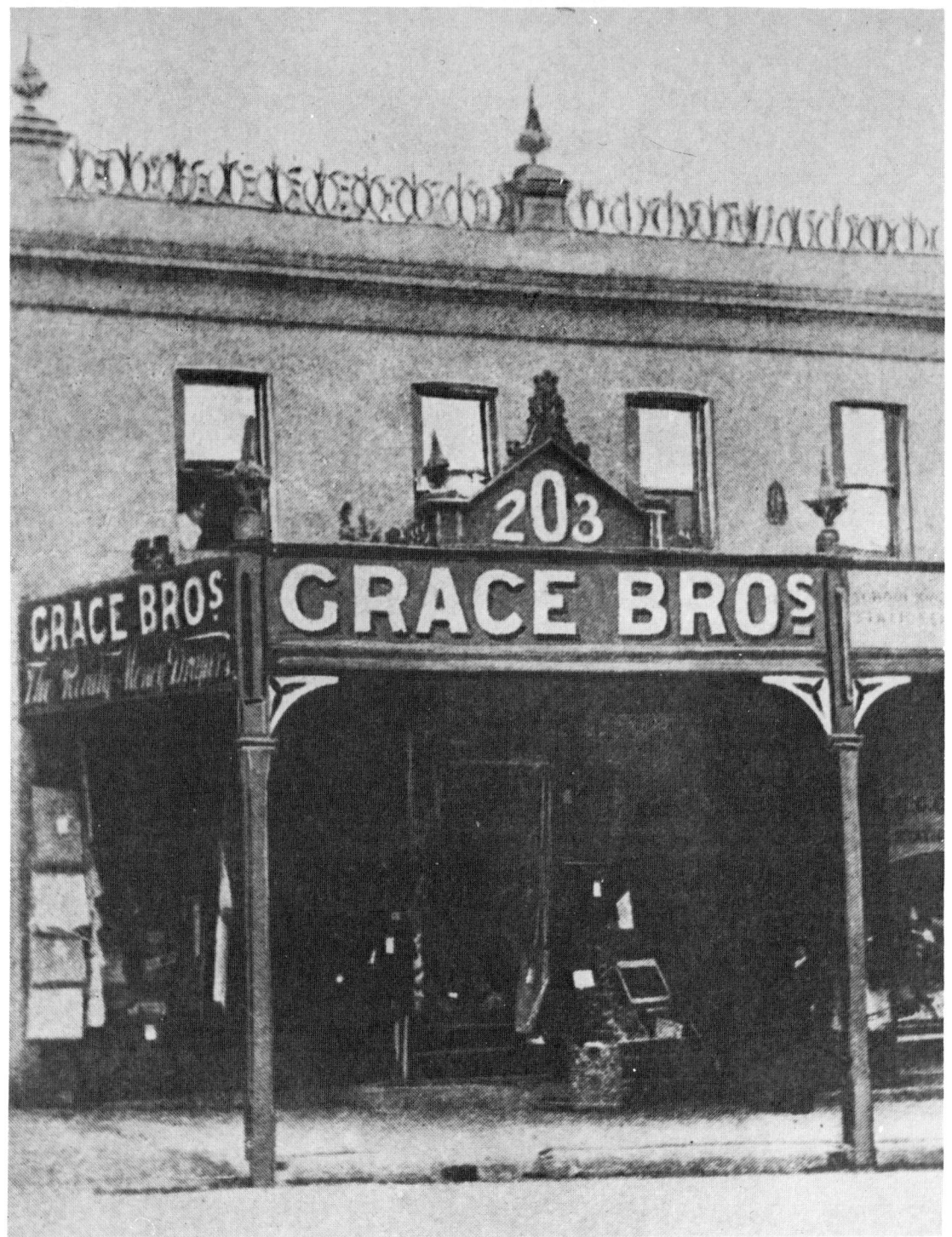

99] Grace Bros. original shop at 203 George Street West (now Broadway), which opened in 1885. Their choice of these premises came about through the purchase of a new collar by Albert Edward Grace. Entering the shop, the brothers found it dingy and untidy, and Albert had to climb a ladder to get the collar. The owner, an old lady, told them she wanted to retire. They offered to buy the business and she accepted. Born in Buckinghamshire, England, the Grace brothers served their apprenticeships in London shops. Joseph came to Sydney, his first job being at Farmer's. Albert went to Canada, then the United States. Joseph later sent for him, and they became partners, selling drapery from a horse and cart. Their partnership was life long.

100] Albert Edward Grace

101] Joseph Neal Grace

102] Some early removal vans

103] Mrs. Anthony Hordern (1792-1871)
above

104] Anthony Hordern (1788-1869)
right

105] Anthony Hordern & Sons, "Universal Providers", whose department store was spread over four large buildings at George Street, Haymarket, before fire gutted three of them and severely damaged a fourth, in 1901. At the left of the rear building was the Australian Gas Light Company's city gasometer.
below

106] Hordern's on fire, 10th July, 1901. George Street was blocked off, tram services diverted, and all city firemen, as well as Railway and suburban volunteers attended. But they were powerless against a strong south-westerly wind.

107] The Exhibition Building, Prince Alfred Park (demolished), where Sam Hordern set up business after the fire, with stock from the firm's bulk and reserve warehouses. Business competitors offered him help with goods and premises.

108] *left* John L. Hordern, grandson of the original Anthony Hordern.

109] *centre* Rebecca Carr, wife of Edward Hordern.

110] *right* Edward Hordern, John Hordern's partner.

111] *below* Hordern Brothers department store, 211 Pitt Street, near King Street, about 1880. The firm came into being in 1870 as a partnership between John and Edward Hordern and their younger brother, Alfred

112] *top* Nock & Kirby's first shop, 194 George Street, near Circular Quay, about 1903. Sydney-born Thomas Nock started work here in 1873 at the age of 13 in the employ of Frederick Felton, ironmonger. Felton took him into partnership in 1884, and the firm became Felton & Nock. In 1894, Joseph Kirby, a young Englishman with hardware experience was introduced to Nock, who wanted a business partner. So came into being Nock & Kirby, one of Sydney's oldest hardware retailers. The two men remained partners all their lives.

lower left 113] Thomas Nock *lower right* 114] Joseph Kirby

115] Way's general drapery store, 263-265 Pitt Street, in the 1890s. Way's were in business in Sydney in the 1860s, when Mrs. Way ran a milliner's at 418 George Street. In 1864 she moved into Pitt Street, and in 1889 the firm became E. Way & Company.

116]

Francis Foy, at the age of 21.

117] The first Mark Foy shop in Sydney, opened in 1885 in Oxford Street, almost at the corner of Hyde Park, by Francis Foy. His father, Mark Foy, died in 1870.

118]

Some early delivery vans of Mark Foy's.

DISASTERS, EVENTS, & OCCASIONS

119] E. W. O'Sullivan turning the first sod, Gladesville, 1901, for the Field of Mars tramway. Mr. G. E. Herring declared that the residents had been euchred out of the tram for years, but now the Minister was going to "lead spades". Mr. O'Sullivan replied that it was the beginning of a tram line that would go through to Woolwich. After three hearty cheers all sat down to a banquet in the local Drill Hall.

The University of Sydney under construction: two photographs taken (probably in 1859) by John Smith, first Professor of Chemistry and Experimental Physics.

120] *top*

A stonemason carves a decorative gargoyle. Professor Smith is at right, wearing his black stove-pipe hat, watch in hand, timing the exposure of a slow wet-plate collodion negative.

121] *left*

Part of a view of one of the doorways of the Great Hall. Professor Smith, wearing a different stove-pipe hat, times the exposure leaning against Hudson's builder's ladder.

122] *above*
Labor Day in Sydney, October, 1908. The annual Eight-Hours' Procession makes its way down Park Street.

123] *right*
The horseless carriage moves into party politics—bringing lady voters to the polling booth.

124] Sir Henry Parkes (1815-1896) lays the foundation stone of the Sydney Trades Hall on the building site at Goulburn and Dixon Streets, in 1888. He was then Premier of New South Wales. The following year he laid the foundation stone of Sydney's Australia Hotel (*see* No. 167) at the other end of the city, and the social scale.

125] *above* The Garden Palace of the Sydney International Exhibition, 1879, built in the Domain near Macquarie Street. The first international exhibition held in Australia, it attracted entries from all States and from many overseas countries.

126] *below* The Garden Palace burnt down, 1882. Much of the work done on the Census of 1881 was destroyed during the fire, although according to Sydney folk-lore it conveniently removed certain convict records.

127] A motor reliability trial starts from Sydney Town Hall, 1905. Of 35 entrants in heavy cars, light cars, and on motor-cycles, only 22 reached Melbourne. Bad roads caused a number of breakdowns, one car being carried into Albury on the back of a motor lorry.

128] Watching the Soudan Contingent leave, East Circular Quay, 1885. The force was offered to Great Britain by the Acting Premier, William Bede Dalley, on the death of General Gordon at Khartoum. It consisted of a six-gun battery with 212 men, 522 infantry, and 200 horses, and was commanded by Colonel J. S. Richardson. The contingent sailed for Africa on 3rd March.

However, Parliament had not been consulted about raising and equipping the troops, and on 17th March the Legislative Assembly had to grant the government an indemnity for its actions. Enlisting soldiers for service overseas was claimed to be unconstitutional. Sir Henry Parkes came out of retirement to win an election on the issue. The contingent did hardly any actual fighting.

129] *above* A shipment of Fiji bananas lands in Sydney, 1909. Thousands of bunches of the large "Fijian Queens" arrived every month during their season.

130] *below* The Chess Championship of Australia, 1913. The defending champion, W. S. Viner, a Bellingen farmer, plays Dr. Lancaster, of Kempsey, with referee David Sands at the Sydney School of Arts Chess Club.

131] *above*
The fire-float *Pluvius* and its water-tenders fight a big fire in a timber yard on Blackwattle Bay in 1905.

132] *below*
Land auction at Sydenham, 1884. In a "Clearance Sale" of the Marionette Estate 54 allotments were offered, all Torrens title, on the afternoon of Saturday, 2nd February, on "Wonderfully Easy Terms". The Estate was bounded by Unwin's Bridge Road, Lymerston Street, Cook's River Road (now Prince's Highway), and Belmore Road.

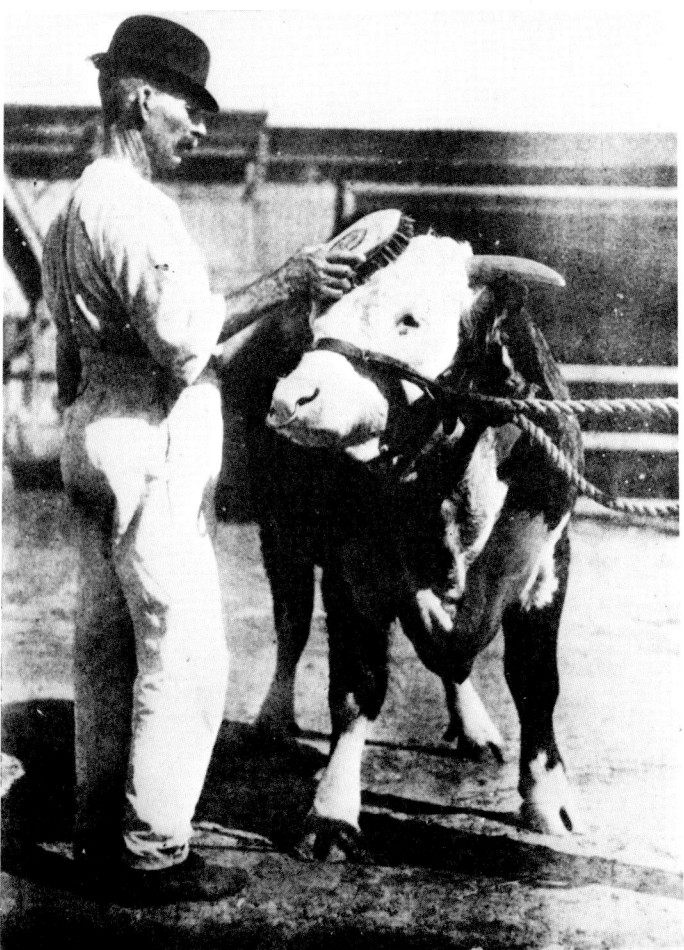

The Easter Show, 1914

133] *top*
Exercising a Clydesdale draught horse for his ring event.

134] *below*
Getting ready for the judges. Grooming a Hereford bull.

SYDNEYSIDERS AT WORK

135] *top*   Willoughby volunteer firemen with equipment, outside their station, about 1905.

136] *lower*   Chatswood volunteer firemen, about 1900. Their first call was to a blaze in a shed containing three tons of onions.

"Fish is about the dearest thing one can buy," a journalist wrote in 1909. He went on to say that it was one of the most extraordinary features of the food supply of Sydney, although the ocean was at the City's very door. "The cost of fish is an eye-opener, and for citizens of limited means a fish meal becomes a luxury."

137] *top*   Early morning net fishermen at Bondi Beach.

138] *lower*   Prawning in Sydney Harbour.

The Fish Markets, Woolloomooloo, 1904

139] *top*
Making a deal in lobsters and smoked fish.

140] *centre*
Fish is inspected for cold storage.

141] *lower*
Fish cleaners at work.

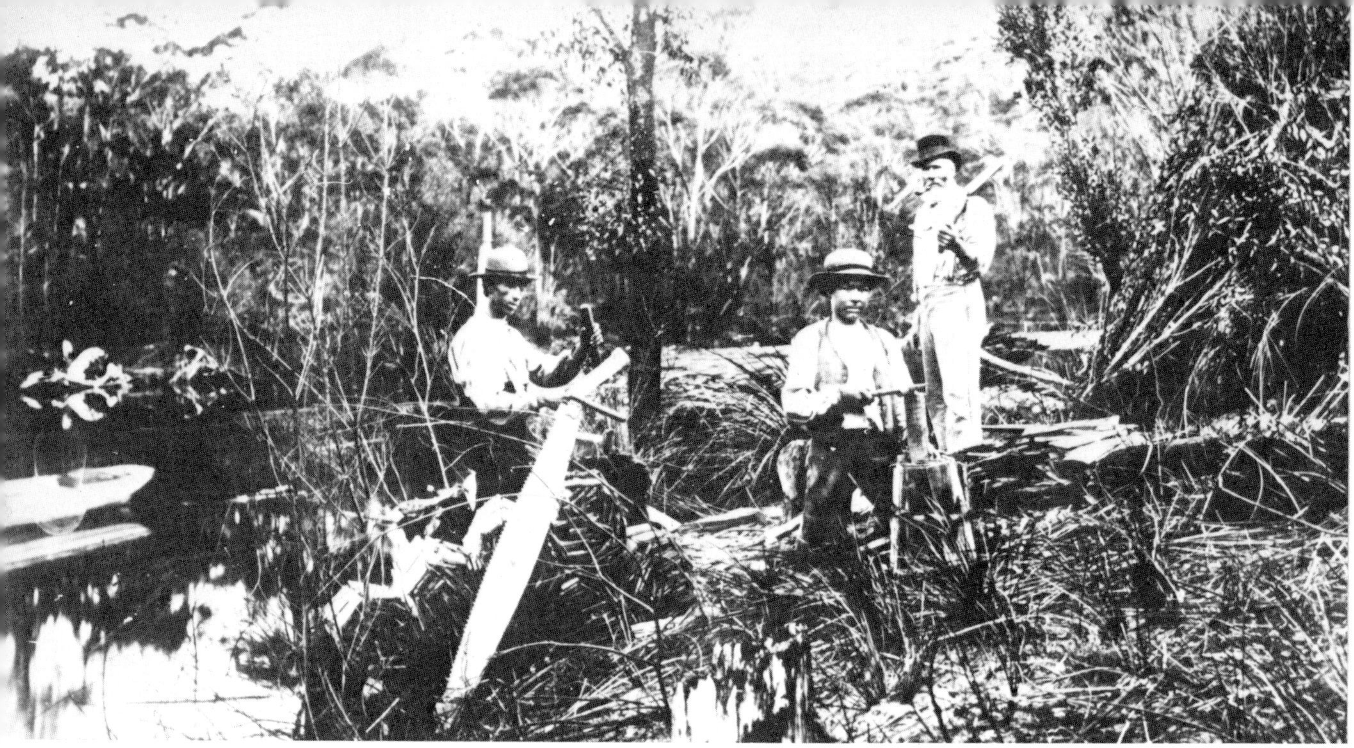

142] *top* Shingle-splitters in the bush, up Middle Harbour way.

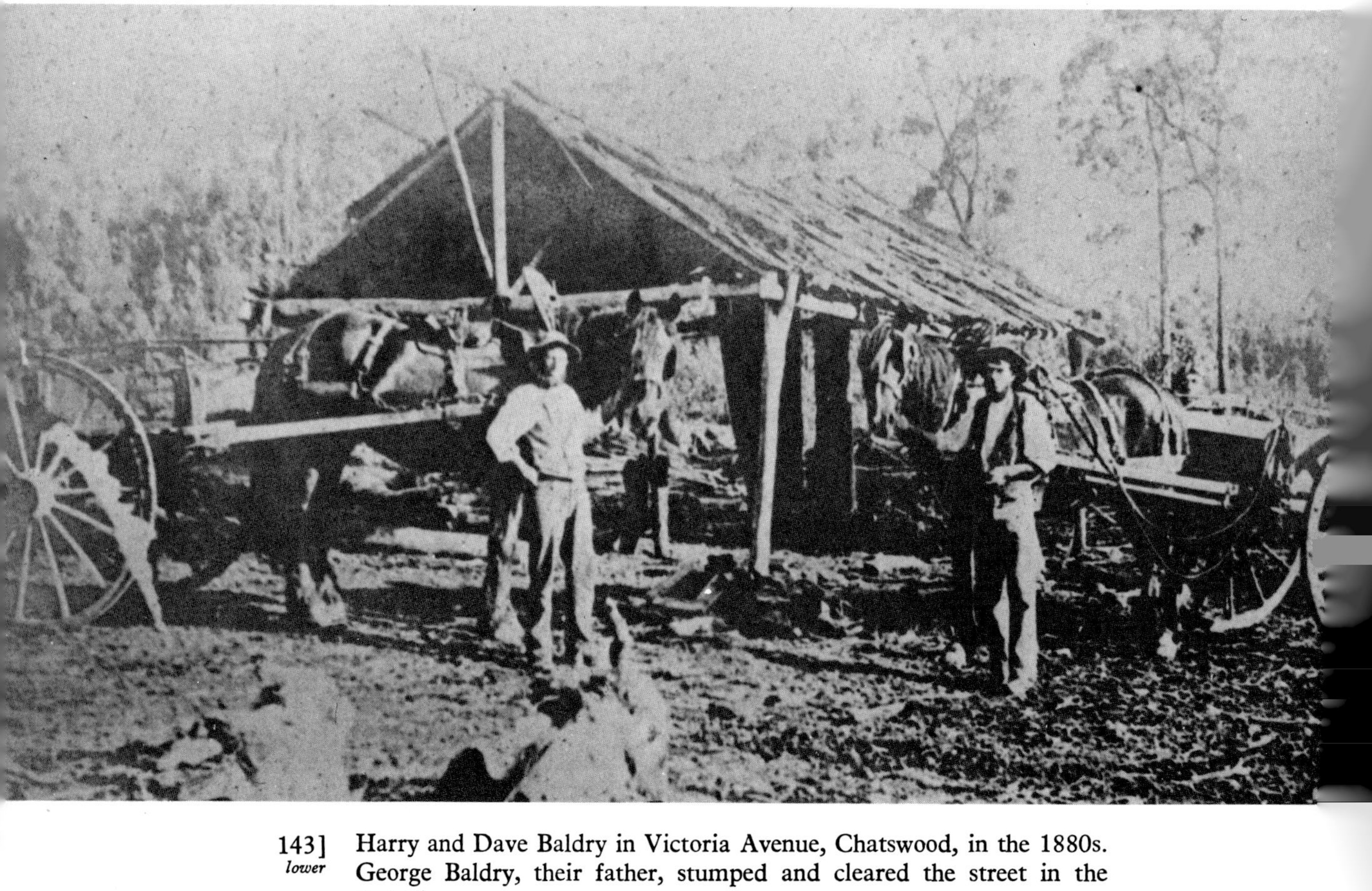

143] *lower* Harry and Dave Baldry in Victoria Avenue, Chatswood, in the 1880s. George Baldry, their father, stumped and cleared the street in the first place.

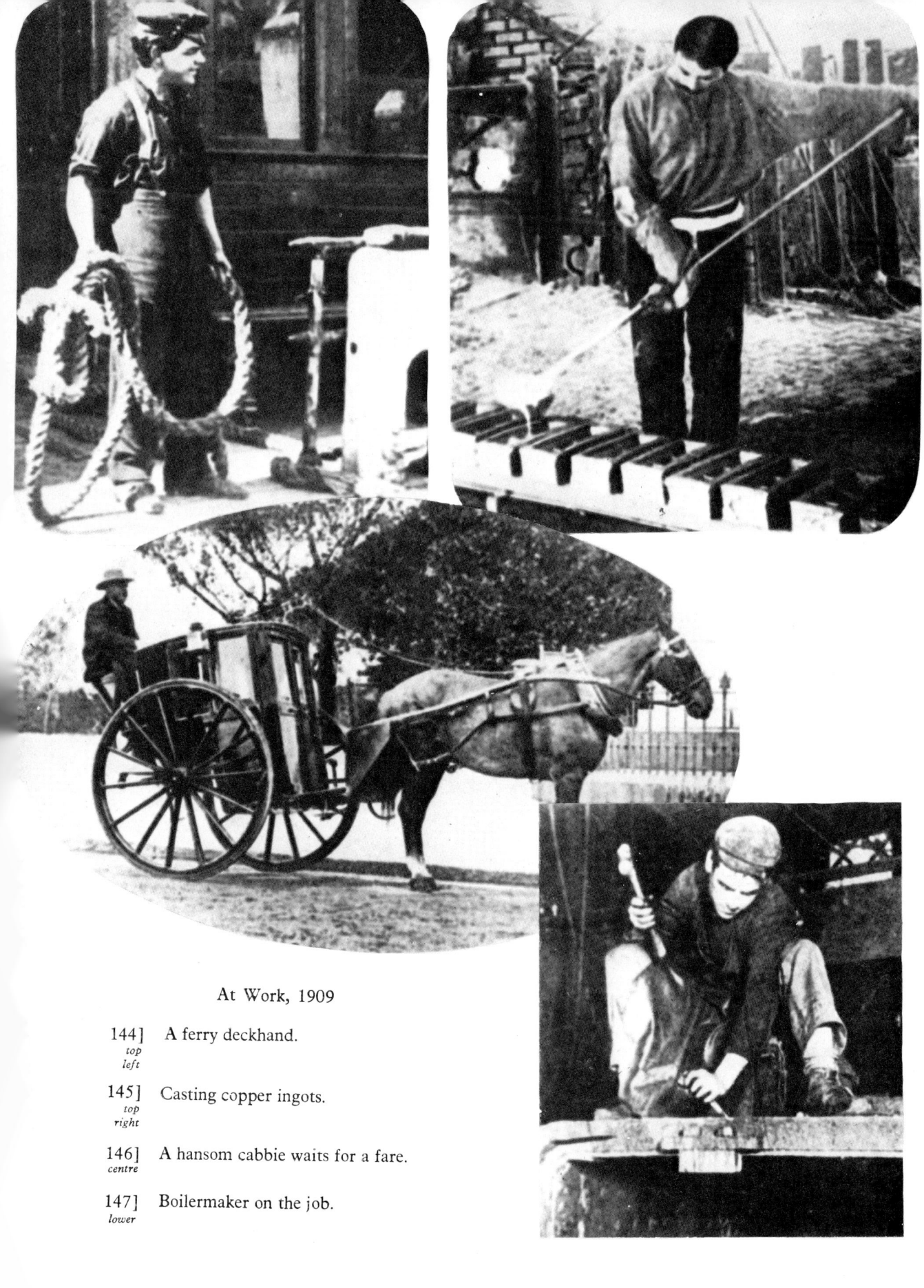

At Work, 1909

144] *top left*   A ferry deckhand.

145] *top right*   Casting copper ingots.

146] *centre*   A hansom cabbie waits for a fare.

147] *lower*   Boilermaker on the job.

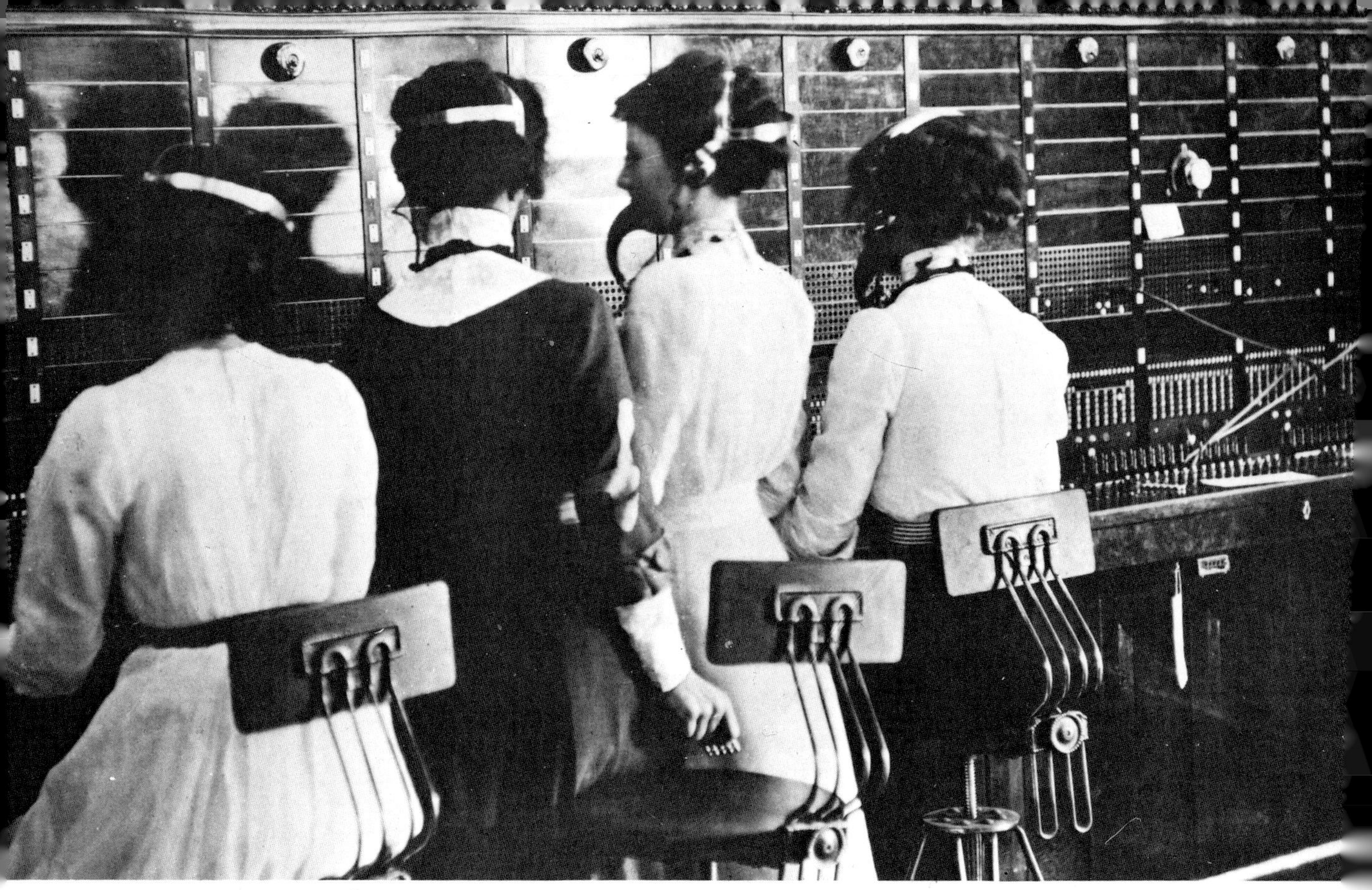

148] *top* Switchgirls operating the manual telephone exchange.

149] *lower* Laying underground telephone cables in Bridge Street, Sydney, 1910.

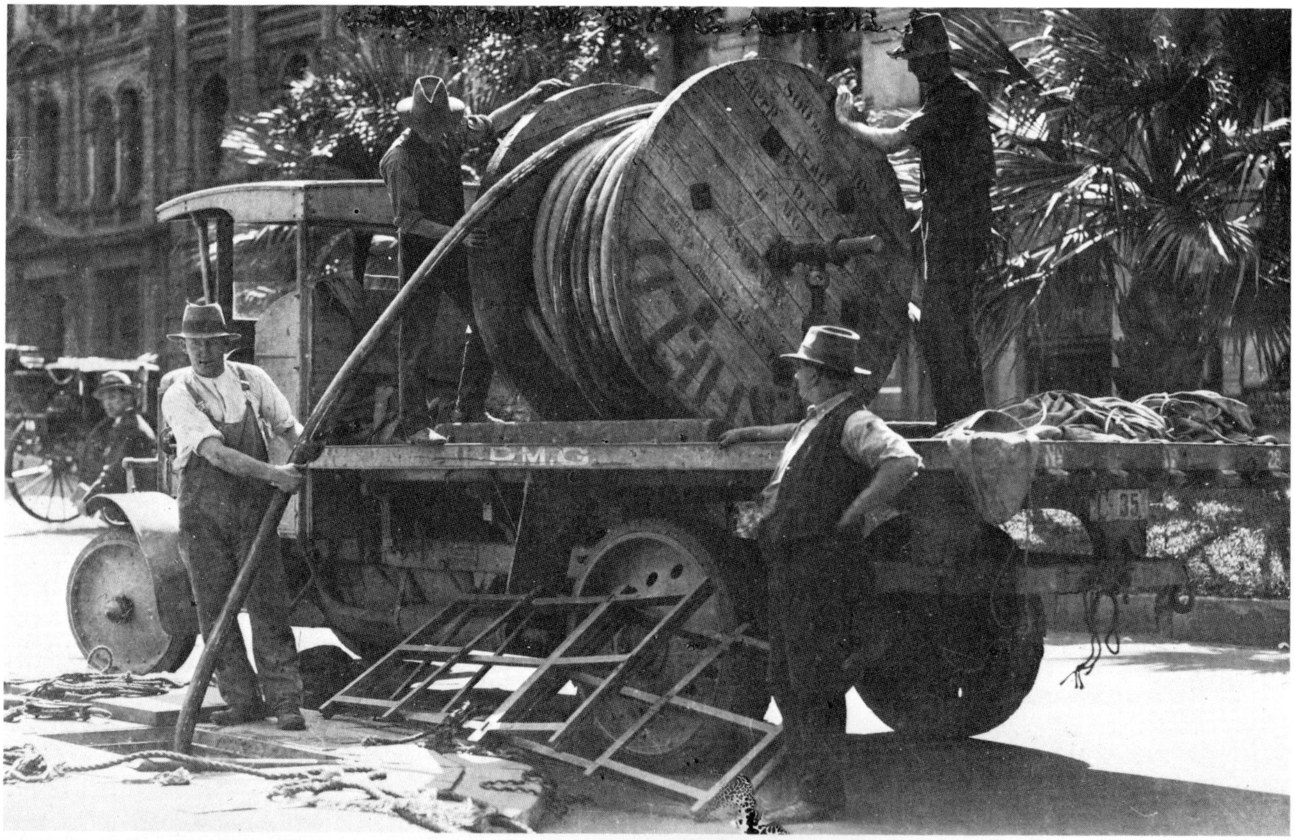

150] Linesmen maintaining the city telephone system before the wires went underground. Sydney before the first World War was heavily forested with poles of all kinds: telephone, telegraph, electricity supply, and tramway power cable; unsightly in appearance, but essential to the public services that the city needed.

151] *left*
Dick Manning, Post Office mounted messenger, about 1890.

152] *below*
Sorting letters at the Sydney G.P.O., before the first World War.

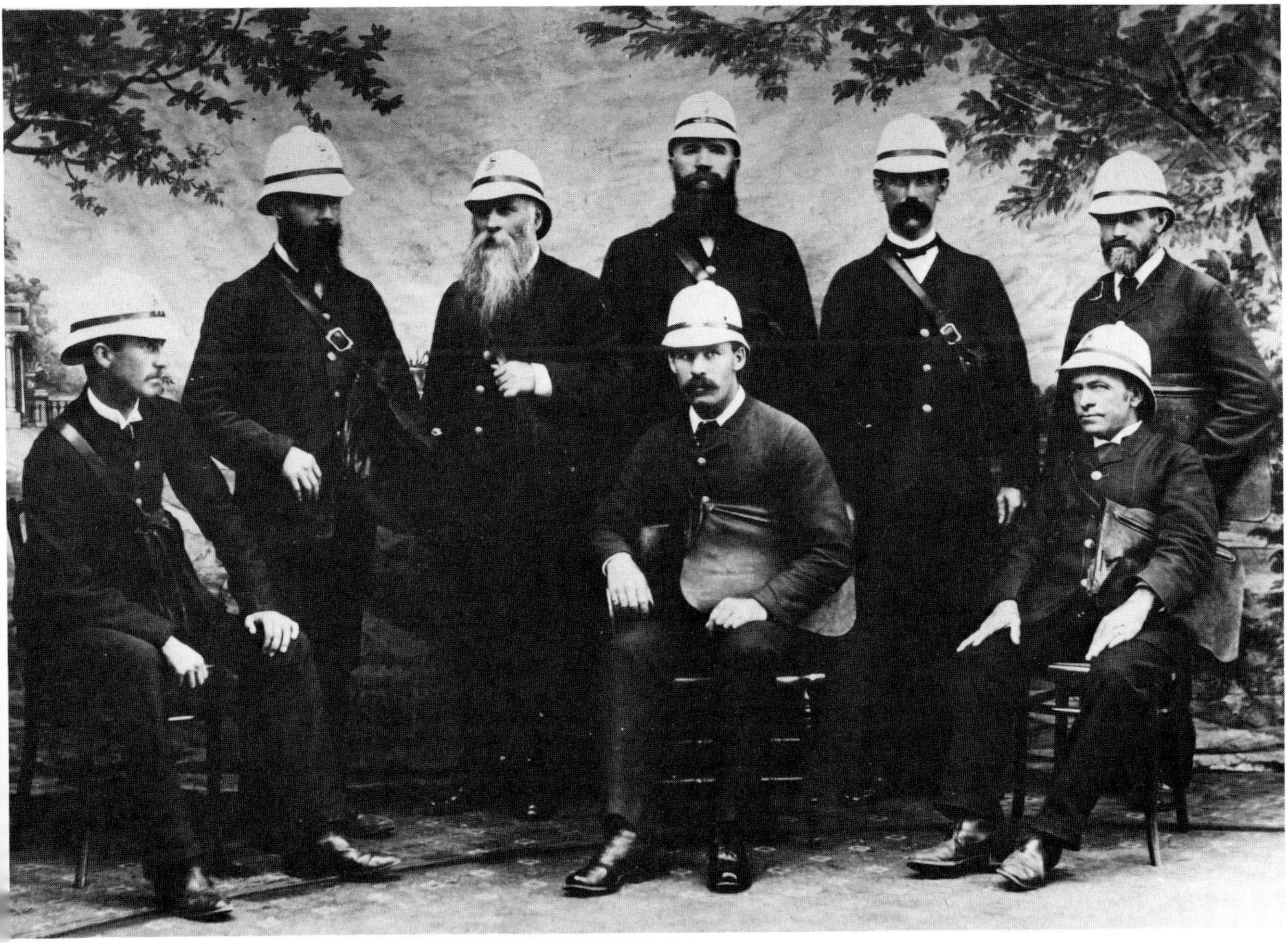

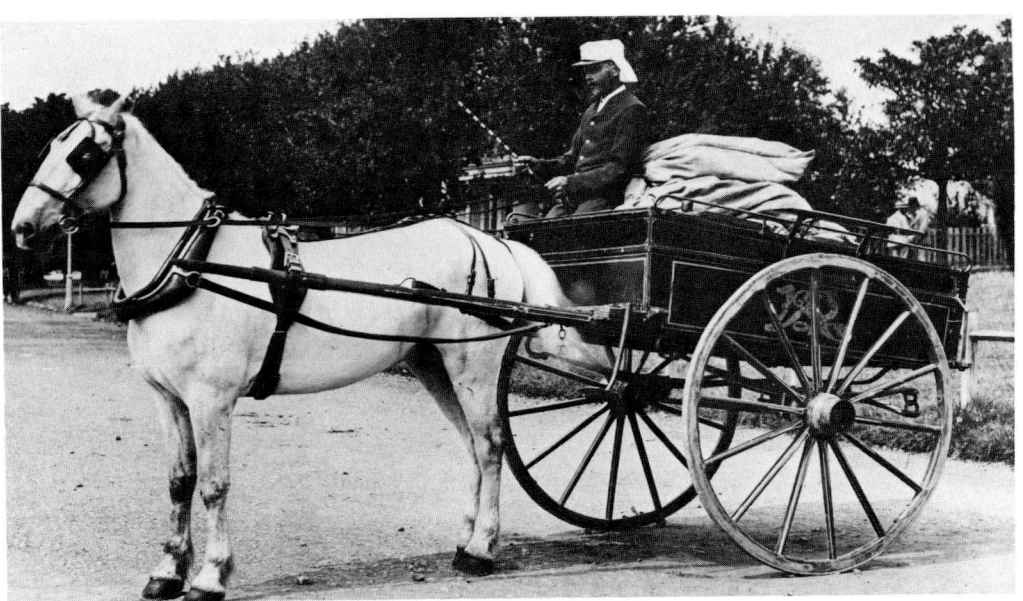

153] *top* A group of postmen about 1890.

154] *lower* A Sydney mail cart used in the 1890s.

Wharf Labourers, 1909

155] *above* Leaving the Oddfellows' Temple, Elizabeth Street, City, after a meeting that decided not to go on strike.

156] *below* Wharf labourers at lunch—serving out tea.

157] The blacksmith and his striker at work at their portable forge on the deck of a sailing ship in port, 1910. A ship's running gear was just as subject to wear and tear as any other kind of machinery; sailors could carry out repairs on wire and ropework, but the blacksmith was needed to maintain chains and other heavy ironwork.

THEATRES, HOTELS, PUBS

158] An Edwardian theatre audience, probably in the Palace Theatre, Pitt Street. One of George Adams's many interests, it was built in 1896. Demolished, of course.

159] Prince of Wales Theatre, Castlereagh Street, near King Street, after the fire, 1872. A full house the previous night had seen *The House that Jack Built*, now the same cast had no stage at all. The alarm was raised about half-past three in the morning, but firemen were helpless. The building was not insured, nor were the costumes, properties, or musical instruments. The fire probably started in the property-room, where chemicals used for stage effects were stored.

160] Harry Rickards' Tivoli Theatre, Castlereagh Street, near King Street, 1906.

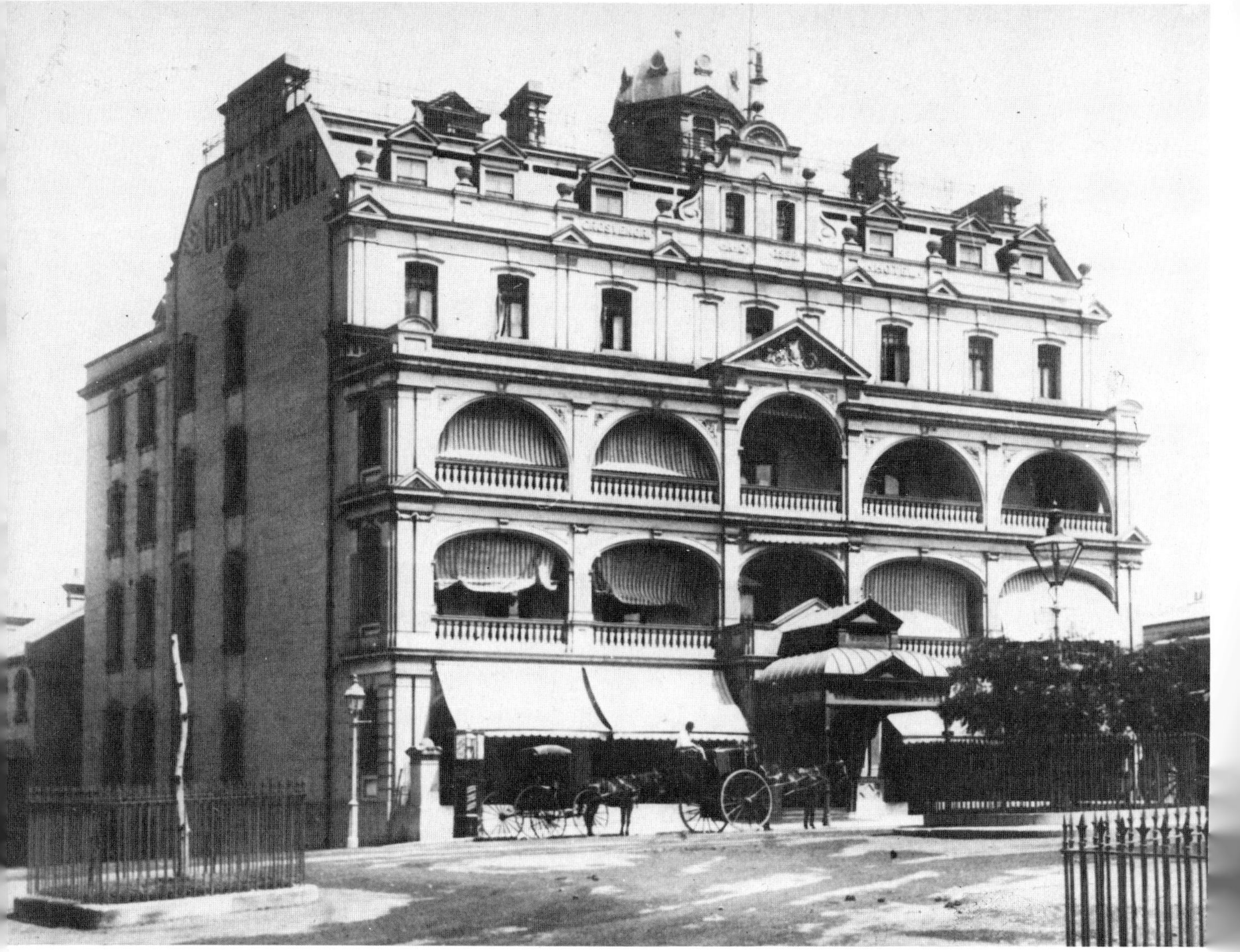
GROSVENOR

WHALERS
ARMS

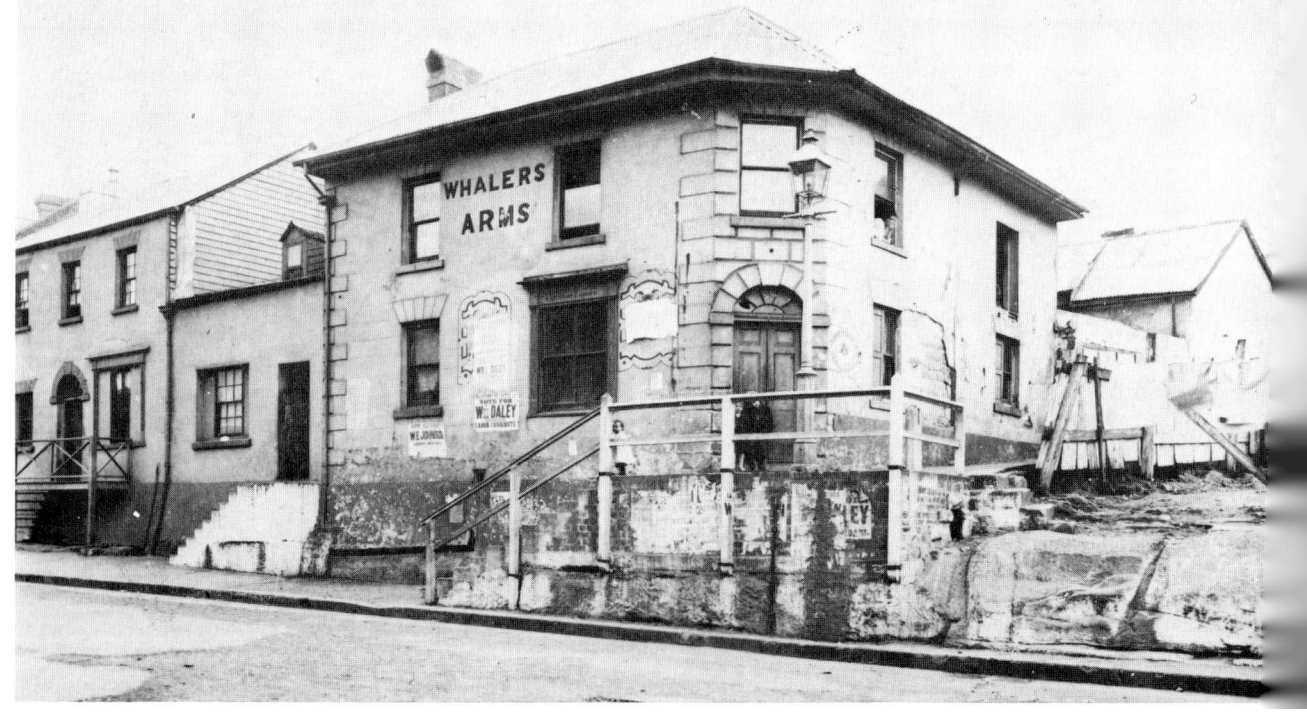

161] *opposite top* — The Grosvenor Hotel on the summit of Church Hill stood in an area that has undergone extensive changes. It was said to be designed in the Queen Anne style.

162] *opposite lower* — The Whaler's Arms, a Rocks' pub from earlier times.

163] *above* — Hotel Metropole, Phillip and Bent Streets, opened in 1890, and described by the *Sydney Morning Herald* as "the high-water mark of the year's advance in city improvement". Built for the Australian Coffee Palace Company, it was lit by electricity generated with its own dynamos. The *Herald*, calling its architectural style Italian renaissance, gushed: "no more magnificent structure in design and appointment can be found in the colonies....". Generations of Sydneysiders liked the old Metropole, and it was popular with country people.

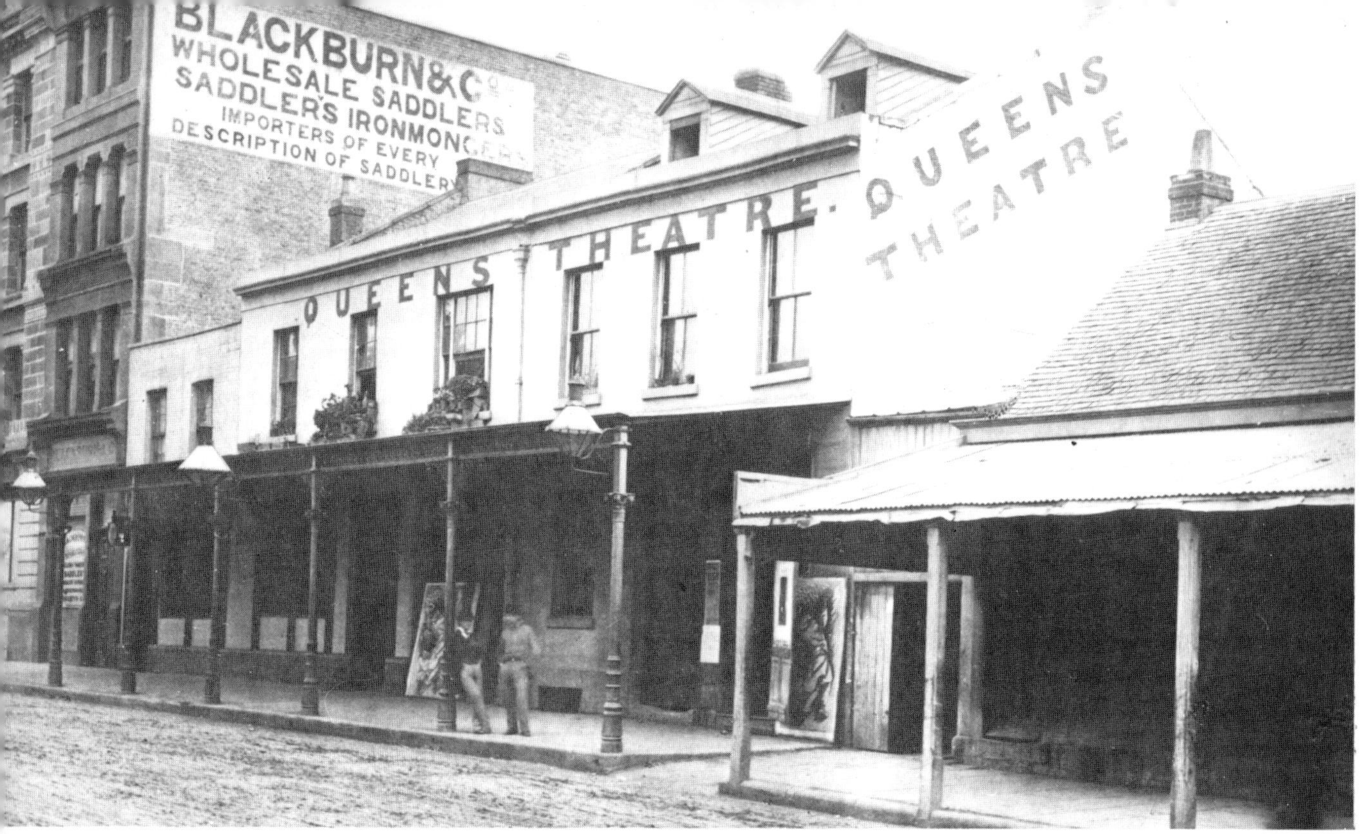

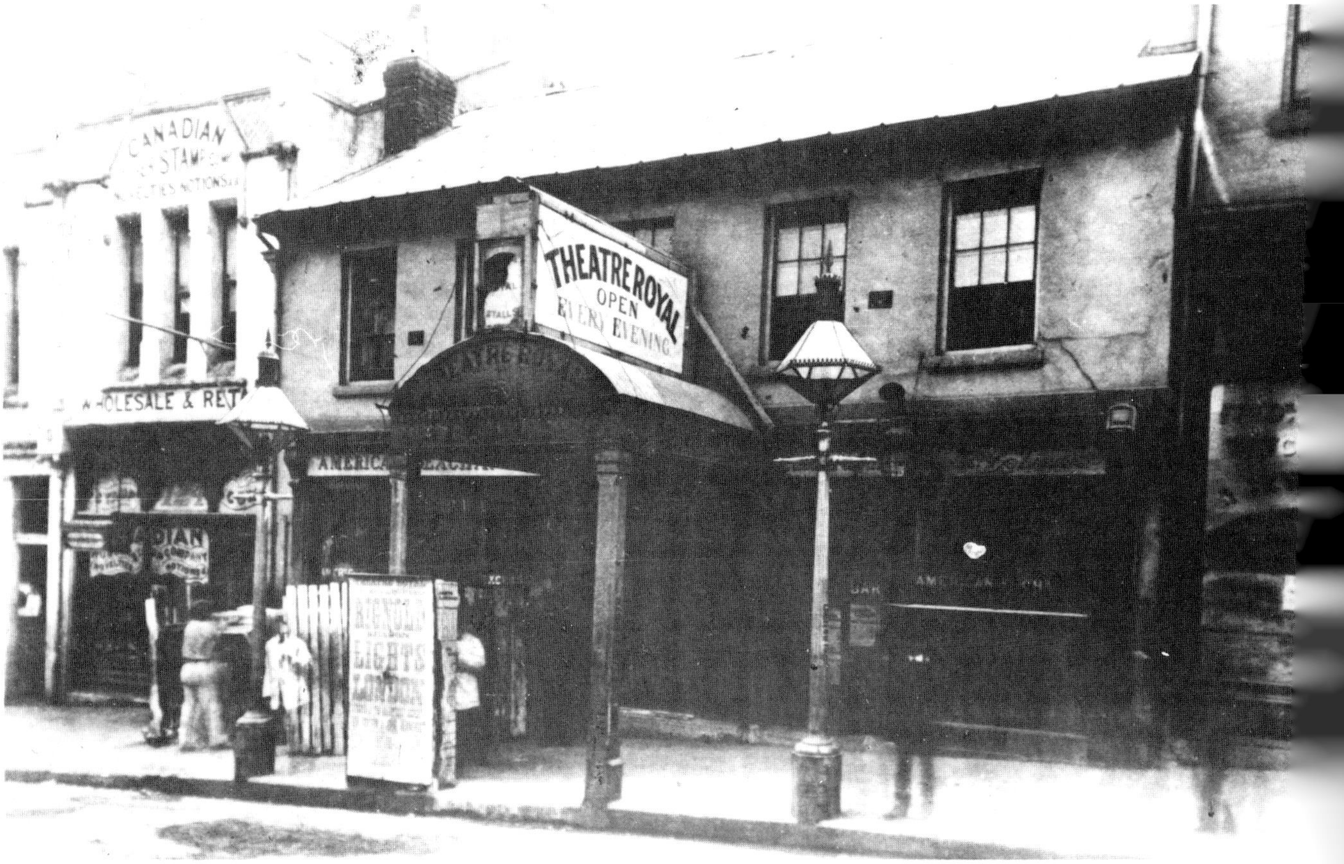

164] *top* Queen's Theatre, 151 York Street, between King and Market Streets.

165] *below* Theatre Royal stalls entrance, King Street, 1880s.

166] The ornate Gaiety Theatre, at 205 Castlereagh Street.

167] *right*

The Australia Hotel (since demolished), Castlereagh Street, near Martin Place, once the largest palace hotel in the Colonies. At a ceremony in 1889, the Premier, Sir Henry Parkes, said that his friends in the temperance bodies might be alarmed at his laying the foundation stone of a hotel, but he supposed that he would be able to justify it, as he had to justify many other acts. He recollected a time when there was only one small coffee-house in Sydney, denoted by "a brown loaf, a pumpkin, and a pound of uncooked steak in the window".

168] *below*

Richard Loseby was licensee of The Packhorse Hotel, 20 Campbell Street, Sydney, in the 1860s.

PUBLIC TRANSPORT

169] A north-bound passenger train emerges from Waverton Tunnel in the days of steam power. The North Shore railway line was originally a suburban extension from Hornsby; a single track to St. Leonards in 1890, and an extension to Milson's Point in 1893. Most of the services were local, and the timetable fitted in with the Circular Quay ferries. There were no Sunday trains until 1893. A government official once declared that it would be better to tear up the rails than extend the line to Milson's Point.

170] Steam trams pass each other in Elizabeth Street, Sydney.

171] Changing over at Edgecliff, about 1900. Cable trams from King Street, Sydney, met the electric service from Dover Road, Rose Bay, at Ocean Street.

172] It was all smiles at the official opening of the Arncliffe Station to Bexley steam tramway service in 1909.

173] George Street, Sydney, 1909. A coal strike that curtailed electric tram services caused this dire overloading.

174] *top* Hansom cabs in Elizabeth Street, outside the old Registrar-General's Department (now offices attached to the Supreme Court).

175] *below* A steam tram at Woollahra.

176] The ferry for Fig Tree entering the Lane Cove River, between Woolwich and lower Greenwich.

177] The paddle-wheeler *Fairlight* on a voyage to Manly Beach.

A FEW SYDNEYSIDERS

178] Mrs. John Harris, wife of the Mayor of Sydney, in 1883, when she laid the foundation stone of the Centennial Hall of Sydney Town Hall. She is wearing a formal black satin day dress embroidered with black lace trimming, hung with jet beads.

179] *top left*
Mrs. Quong Tart.

180] *above*
Quong Tart (1850-1903), business man, mine-owner, tea and silk merchant, restaurateur, and "unpaid Consul-General for China", came to New South Wales at the age of nine. He grew up in Braidwood and made successful gold-mining speculations, and married Margaret Scarlett (top left) in Sydney in 1886. Quong Tart was a popular and influential Sydneysider, his tea-rooms were highly successful; he was a good employer, a generous giver, and became well-known for his renditions of Scottish songs. He was twice decorated by the Chinese government. But he could not persuade the N.S.W. Government to ban opium, on which heavy import duties were levied.

181] *left*
Fusajiro Kanematsu (1845-1913), the pioneer Japanese merchant in Australia, came here in 1888 and in 1890 established F. Kanematsu Ltd. He died in Kobe, Japan. The Kanematsu Memorial Institute at Sydney Hospital was established in 1933 by the firm to perpetuate the memory of Kanematsu and his wife, Sen.

182] David Scott Mitchell, founder of the Mitchell Library.

183] *right* Sir Henry Parkes, in old age.

184] *below* W. F. King, "The Flying Pieman", marathon walker.

185] Sydney-born Nellie Stewart, darling of the theatre for half a century.

186]   Mr. and Mrs. Samuel Hordern.

187]   Andrew Torning, volunteer fireman.

188]   Joseph Fowles, street directory pioneer.

189]   Edwin Whitfield, noted Sydney Grammar School teacher.

190] O'Donovan's Castle, Darling Point, 1890. Dubbed "an Australian Diogenes", Harry O'Donovan lived in a quiet corner off the "Breakneck Steps" that led to Double Bay, not far from St. Mark's Church. A good neighbour, he became the local night watchman. Fortunately for Harry there was then no local government by-law to regulate eccentricity in architecture.

191] George Robertson (1860-1933) founded, with David Angus, the long established Sydney booksellers and publishers. He was born at Halstead, Essex, and trained as a bookseller in Glasgow. Best-selling authors published by him included Lawson, Dennis, and Paterson, but he also took on works of merit with little profit in them.

192] Yesterday's little girls pose in their Sunday best: studio portraits by Freeman Brothers, "photographists", of George Street.

193] Four studio portraits of little boys all dressed up and told to keep still while Freeman Brothers took their photograph.

194] Some of the kids whose playgrounds were the back lanes and side streets of places like Chippendale, Darlinghurst, or the Rocks.

195] "Children Taken Instantaneously": Freeman Brothers' advertisement in *Sands' Sydney Directory* for 1863.

196] Sturdy barefoot boys, their dogs, and little girls minding Baby: young Sydneysiders in the back streets of 1902.

197] A popularity of pinafores in an Edwardian backyard.

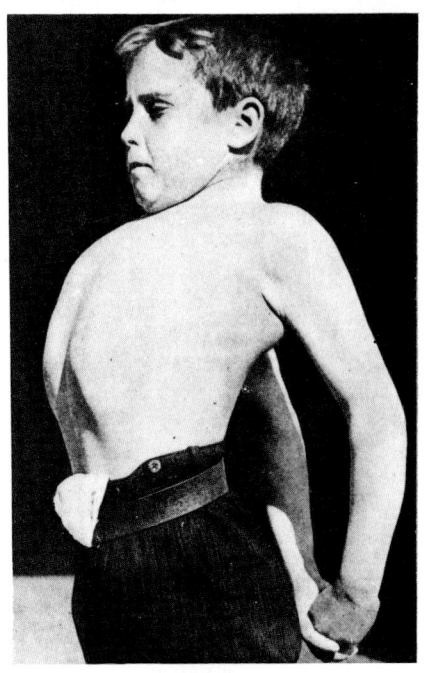

198] Chest development exercises at Fort Street Primary School, 1913. The physical training programme at the school was in the charge of Major A. W. Parsonage, and included organized games held every second Friday in the Domain, or at Centennial Park, Paddington. Handkerchief parades were also held, to encourage their use.

199] John Smith (1821-1885), first Professor of Chemistry and Experimental Physics at the University of Sydney, and a pioneer photographer of the 1850s. Born at Peterculter, Aberdeenshire, Scotland, he became a leader of scientific progress in the Colony, and had wide interests. He was one of the earliest users of the wet-plate collodion process.

Goodbye, Sydney Town, Sydney Town, goodbye,
  I am leaving you today for a country far away.
Though just now I'm stony broke, without a single brown,
  When I make my fortune, I'll come back
To dear old Sydney Town.

—From a Diggers' song, first World War.